NAME THAT BOOK!

Questions and Answers on Outstanding Children's Books

by JANET GREESON
and KAREN TAHA

The Scarecrow Press, Inc.
Metuchen, N.J., & London
1986

The graphics used as illustrations in Chapter VII are courtesy of two Macintosh programs: "Click Art" from T/Maker Graphics, 2115 Landings Dr., Mountain View, CA 94043, and "McPic" from Magnum Software, 2115 Devonshire St., Ste. 337, Chatsworth, CA 91311. Used by permission.

Library of Congress Cataloging-in-Publication Data

Greeson, Janet, 1952–
    Name that book!

    Includes indexes.
    1. Children's literature--Miscellanea.
2. Educational games. 3. Literary recreations.
I. Taha, Karen T. II. Title.
PN1009.A1G715 1986   809'.89282   86-10207
ISBN 0-8108-1908-2

To Jim and Helen

J. G.

To Hamdy

K. T.

CONTENTS

PREFACE

NAME THAT BOOK! was written primarily for elementary and junior high/middle school library media specialists, classroom teachers, and anyone else interested in getting kids into good books. It takes the work out of launching your own game show of Battle of Books, providing ammunition (the questions), and rules and suggestions on how to have a successful game. We have also included additional activities to spark interest in reading and make the library media center an exciting gathering spot for children and, more importantly, a place where learning is sure to take place.

Battle of Books has been played in schools and libraries since the 1940's, when it was a weekly feature on a Chicago Public Schools' radio program. Recently the game has experienced a resurgence of popularity, primarily due to the article, "'Battle of Books' Urbana Style," by Joanne Kelly in School Library Journal, October, 1982.

We have been holding Battle of Books competitions in our respective schools for four years. From the outset, the excitement and enthusiasm generated by the game convinced us of its value in meeting one of the primary goals of the library media program--that of bringing children and good books together.

Soon after deciding to begin Battle of Books, however, we discovered how difficult and time-consuming it was to gather enough questions for even one session. The only books available which expressly fit that purpose were two by Ruth Harshaw, WHAT BOOK IS THAT? (Macmillan, 1948), and IN WHAT BOOK? (Macmillan, 1970). Both of these books are out of print and include no books published after 1968.

Out of necessity we began the long process of compiling our own question files, emphasizing recognized favorites, classics, award winners, and recommended titles published since 1970. This file has finally become NAME THAT BOOK!

Titles were selected for inclusion in NAME THAT BOOK! on the premise that Battle of Books should encourage reading of the best available literature for children and, at the same time, include those books most likely to be in an elementary or junior high/middle school library media center.

Sources for selection were the following:

School Library Journal, Best Books Lists, 1970-1984
ALA Notable Books, 1970-1984
Elementary School Library Collection, 1982
Children's Catalog, 1981 edition and 1982, 1983, 1984 supplements
Newbery Award winners and honor books
Caldecott Award winners and honor books
National Book Awards
State Award Lists, including:
    Arkansas--Charlie May Simon Award
    California--Young Reader Medal
    Colorado Children's Book Award
    Florida--Sunshine State Award
    Georgia Children's Book Award
    Georgia Children's Picture Storybook Award
    Indiana--Young Hoosier Award
    Iowa--Children's Choice Award
    Hawaii--Nene Award
    Kansas--William Allen White Children's Book Award
    Massachusetts Children's Book Award
    Missouri--Mark Twain Award
    Ohio--Buckeye Children's Book Award
    Oklahoma--Sequoyah Children's Book Award
    Nebraska--Golden Sower Reading Program
    Pacific Northwest Library Association Young Reader Choice Award (Alaska, Washington, Oregon, Montana, Idaho, British Columbia)
    South Carolina Children's Book Award and Young Adult Book Award
    Tennessee Children's Choice Book Award
    Texas Bluebonnet Award
    Vermont--Dorothy Canfield Fisher Children's Book Award
    West Virginia Children's Book Award

After determining specific titles to be included, we divided the list, read the books and wrote three questions for each title. The questions were traded, double-checked and

revised, always with an eye toward their primary task--
stimulating interest in the book itself. The final results are
NAME THAT BOOK!, a compilation of 1,704 questions (two
questions for each title), and a software disk containing a
third question for each book in grades four and above, which
can be used for individual or group practice.*

Titles in NAME THAT BOOK! are organized according
to difficulty and appropriateness of material, realizing that,
as individuals and groups differ, you may want to use questions from above or below the actual grade level of the students. Also classics, like fairy tales and folktales, that may
be written at a high reading level but are nevertheless famil-
iar to younger children, are included in the primary grade
level where they are most appropriate.

To assure a fair game, each consecutive pair of questions should be roughly equal in difficulty. For this reason,
questions in NAME THAT BOOK! are organized into suggested
grade levels, with each grade level containing two sections--
"Easier Reading" and "Advanced Reading."

Two questions are included for each title in order to
provide one for practice and another for competition. Letting
children know that they will hear completely new questions
during competitions places the emphasis where it belongs--on
reading the books rather than learning the answers to questions.

Chapter I gives specific suggestions and rules for playing Battle of Books, Chapters II through VI contain the actual questions, and Chapter VII covers a gamut of additional
uses for the questions in NAME THAT BOOK!, from bulletin
boards to "book bees." Author, title, and subject indexes
are included for use in these activities, and to facilitate cor-
relation of reading with school curriculum. As practicing library media specialists, we feel sure that NAME THAT BOOK!
will be a tool that you will use again and again to help build
a vital library media program in your school.

J.G.
K.T.

---

*NAME THAT BOOK! software program for all Apple computers
is available from Scarecrow Press, Inc.

ACKNOWLEDGMENTS

We would like to express our deep appreciation to James Greeson for his support, his invaluable computer expertise, and his unending patience throughout this project.

Thanks are also due to the following people who have contributed in numerous ways to the creation of NAME THAT BOOK!: David V. Loertscher, University of Arkansas; Janet Gibbons and Cheyrl Lyall, Springdale School System; Joan Bachman, Ozarks Regional Library; Jerry Esmail and Fran Rust, American School of Kuwait; and finally the students of Elmdale and Westwood Elementary Schools.

CHAPTER I

BATTLE OF BOOKS: SUGGESTIONS AND RULES

Battle of Books is an ideal activity for elementary and junior high/middle school children because everyone, even the audience, participates. It may be played by a small group, one classroom, or the entire student body. Interschool and community competitions can be a dynamic source of publicity for the library media program, so don't forget to invite parents and the local media to attend, and be sure to videotape the contests for showing at parent-teacher meetings. Practice games may be played throughout the year, while a championship Battle of Books is a fitting finale to Children's Book Week or National Library Week. But you need not wait for a special time. The beauty of Battle of Books is that it creates excitement about reading and books, is readily adaptable to suit diverse groups of children, and provides an opportunity for every student to shine.

Fun games in your own classroom or media center can be as simple as firing questions straight from NAME THAT BOOK! without any special rules or preparations. A class can be divided into any number of teams for a hands-up, no-captain game on the spur of the moment. For those who wish to set up more formal competitions, we provide the following suggestions:

1. Decide on the scope of your Battle of Books--one grade level only? interschool? district-wide? Meet with involved personnel to reserve dates and places for matches. Agree on reading lists to be given to the children or their teachers. We suggest that a comprehensive reading list including titles in two or even three grade levels be distributed early in the school year, not only as a Battle of Books reading list, but as a guide for book reports, recreational reading, and for other suggested activities in NAME THAT BOOK! Any practice

on matching authors and titles should be done with this comprehensive list.

2. Write out--or copy and glue--each question on an index
card or a spare catalog card, with the title and author at the
bottom. The first question listed for each book should be
placed in the practice file, the second in the competition file.
Your question cards should be coded according to grade level
and difficulty, e.g., "4E" for fourth grade easier reading.
You will then have a practice file and a competition file for
each grade level, which you can build upon and use over and
over.

3. Play practice games to familiarize students with pro-
cedures. Playing Battle of Books throughout the school year
facilitates picking your best players as team members for interschool competitions. And more importantly, it gives every
student a chance to be on a team. Let individuals and small
groups play computer Battle of Books with the NAME THAT
BOOK! disk.* You will feel the excitement build as teams are
chosen and competition time draws near.

4. Plan and carry through with publicity needs. This
might include a phone call or letter to the local press and
radio/TV stations, posters, invitations to parents and school
district officials, and videotaping preparations.

5. A week or two before the battle, hold a pre-battle
conference with all library media/teaching staff who are ac-
tively participating in the game. Select questions together
from the competition file. Number them consecutively, beginning with relatively easy questions to give the teams confi-
dence, and making each pair of questions roughly equal in
difficulty. Agree on the specifics of the rules so you can
make them clear to the children. Will the captains be required
to give the exact title, including "The," "A" or "An"? Is it
permissible to mispronounce the author's name? What if the
Game Director hears a team member tell his/her captain the
correct title but the captain repeats it incorrectly? All of
these points need to be clarified to prevent confusion during
a match.

6. Set the stage for Battle of Books by placing two semi-

---

*See Preface

circles of five chairs each at opposite ends of the stage or playing arena. Have on hand: 1) a large clock or timer with a buzzer, 2) a stopwatch for the timekeeper, 3) a chalkboard for keeping score, 4) a podium for the Game Director, with a microphone if needed, and 5) the stack of prepared question cards. Optional additions might be ribbons, medals, paperback books, or trophies as prizes for participants.

RULES FOR PLAYING BATTLE OF BOOKS

EACH TEAM: shall consist of five members, including one captain, who is the sole spokesperson for the team and gives the answer after conferring with teammates. Team members quickly learn to whisper when they confer with one another. The answer is not accepted from any team member other than the captain.

GAME DIRECTOR (library media specialist/teacher): will read each question only once and will be the sole judge of the accuracy of the response. Reading the question only once keeps the players and audience quiet and attentive. It is a good idea for the Game Director to explain the rules of the game to the audience before play begins. This helps parents who are attending, or anyone unfamiliar with Battle of Books, to understand and enjoy the game.

TIME KEEPER (library media specialist/teacher/library aide/parent/student): will give the verbal warning, "Five seconds," fifteen seconds after the reading of the question is completed, and will call "Time," twenty seconds after the reading of the question is completed.

SCORE KEEPER (may be combined with Time Keeper): will tally scores, preferably on a large surface such as a chalkboard, in view of the audience. The score keeper is responsible for tallying scores for three groups: Team A, Team B, and the Audience.

QUESTIONS: Flip a coin to decide which team receives the first question. Questions are given alternately to one team, then the other. In other words, Team A will receive all odd-numbered questions, Team B all even-numbered questions regardless of who has given the previous response. If

the team to whom the question is first directed is unable to
answer correctly within twenty seconds, the other team may
answer, but must do so immediately and without repetition
of the question. Each team gets only one chance to answer
a question correctly. If neither team can answer correctly,
the audience is given an opportunity. No team or audience
may give the author's name before the correct title has been
given.

SCORING: Five points are given for a correct title.
Three additional points are given for the correct last name of
the author. If the first team gives the correct title but not the
author of a book, the second team has the opportunity to earn
three points by naming the correct author (see QUESTIONS).
If both teams fail, the audience has the opportunity (see
AUDIENCE).

AUDIENCE: If neither team can correctly identify the
title and/or author, members of the audience may raise their
hands. The Game Director will then call on up to three people. If a correct response is given, the appropriate score
will be tallied for the audience. The audience gets three
chances to answer correctly because they may NOT confer with
one another before answering.

LENGTH OF GAME: As the match begins, set the timer
for thirty minutes. When the timer sounds, the Game Director
should complete the round in progress, making sure that the
last question is directed to the team initially designated to receive even-numbered questions. A thirty-minute match will
require approximately sixty total questions. Be sure to bring
extra questions, however, as well-read teams will run through
many more questions than you expect within the thirty-minute
period.

Once you launch Battle of Books in your school, it
quickly becomes a focal point of interest. Use this interest
to enhance communication skills as well as to motivate reading. Encourage students to write their own Battle of Books
questions about the books they read by setting up a "Slot
Box" with a supply of blank cards and pencils nearby. Per-
iodically set aside fifteen to thirty minutes for a question-
writing session, but first review the elements of a good question with the class:

1. The question should be specific enough to apply to only one book. For example, a character's name, age, or the setting may be included.

2. The question should relate to a major event or character in the book, incorporating one or more of the "Five W's": who, what, why, when and where.

3. The question should be easy enough to be answered by anyone who has read the book.

4. The question itself should not give away the answer.

Students who write questions good enough to be added to your file should be given credit for their contribution during Battle of Books matches. You may even want to reward their good work with a special certificate or award.

The suggestions and rules delineated above are meant to serve only as guidelines. You may need to adapt them to suit your own circumstances and students. The essential unchanging ingredient of Battle of Books, which will be as rewarding for you as it has been for us, is the interest in good books that this game inspires and the idea that it promotes-- reading is fun!

CHAPTER II

PRIMARY GRADES

EASIER READING

1. A Woggle of Witches by Adrienne Adams
    In what book does a group of witches make a ring
    around the moon and then sit on top of the moon?
    These witches sleep on hammocks high in the trees.
    What is the name of their story?

2. The Crow and the Pitcher by Aesop
    This fable tells about a very thirsty crow who finds a
    pitcher but can't reach the water in the bottom. Do you
    know the title?
    The Sparrow and the Lark won't help the Crow get a
    drink, but he figures out a way. Name that book!

3. The Lion and the Mouse by Aesop
    This fable tells about a mouse who helps a lion in order
    to repay a favor. What is the title?
    The lion is going to kill the mouse, but the mouse talks
    him out of it. What fable is this?

4. Nobody Asked Me If I Wanted a Baby Sister by Martha
    Alexander
    In what book does Oliver try to give away his baby
    sister?
    Name the book in which Oliver gives his baby sister
    to Toby's mom.

5. Sabrina by Martha Alexander
    Sabrina is so unhappy about her name, she runs away
    from school. What is the title of her story?
    When the other children fight over her name, this girl
    decides she will keep it after all. Her name is the title
    of the book. What is it?

6. The Stupids Have a Ball by Harry Allard
   In this book Mrs. Stupid dresses up in some spaghetti. Name that book!
   Cousin Dottie arrives at the Stupids' party wearing a chicken and driving a duck. Can you name this book?

7. The Emperor's New Clothes by Hans Christian Andersen
   This emperor doesn't care about anything but fancy clothes, so he hires two weavers who promise him clothes from magic cloth. Name his story.
   Everyone except a little child is afraid to tell the Emperor that he has no clothes on. What book is this?

8. The Ugly Duckling by Hans Christian Andersen
   All the ducklings hatch out except one big egg, and when it finally hatches, the baby doesn't look at all like the others. Can you name this book?
   The poor duckling who hatches out last is teased and pecked by the other animals. What is the title?

9. Billy and Blaze by C.W. Anderson
   When Billy enters a horse show, he is glad he has practiced jumping fences with his horse. What book is this?
   In what book does Billy get to keep the dog that he freed from a trap?

10. Tim All Alone by Edward Ardizzone
    When Tim arrives home, he finds his parents gone and his house for rent. In what book does he set off to find them?
    Name the book in which Tim gets a job as a cabin boy on the ship Amelia Jane so he can look for his parents.

11. Popcorn by Frank Asch
    In what book is Sam the bear's house filled from top to bottom with popcorn?
    Everyone has a tummyache from eating so much popcorn at Sam's Halloween party. What is the name of the book?

12. Bah! Humbug! by Lorna Balian
    If Margie falls asleep on Christmas Eve, Arthur says he will put ice cubes in her pajamas and bubble gum in her hair. Name that book!

In which book do two children set a trap for Santa with a pail of cold water, string, bells, windchimes and a can of pennies?

13. Animals Should Definitely NOT Wear Clothing by Judi Barrett
    This book shows why it's better that animals don't wear people's clothes. What is the title?
    What is the name of the book that has funny pictures of an elephant in a dress, opossums wearing clothes upside down and a giraffe with seven neckties?

14. Hosie's Alphabet by Leonard Baskin
    Name the alphabet book that shows a colorful animal for each letter, from an armadillo to a zebra.
    What alphabet book has a rhinoceros express and a gangling entangling spider?

15. Oscar Otter by Nathaniel Benchley
    Name the book in which an otter builds a secret slide down the mountain.
    When a moose honks, he scares a fox, a wolf and a mountain lion, and that puts Oscar in great danger. Name that book!

16. The Big Honey Hunt by Stanley and Janice Berenstain
    Porcupines, skunks, owls and angry bees, all make trouble for Small Bear and his dad when they look for a honey tree in this book called....
    In what book do Small Bear and his dad go looking for honey and decide that the best honey comes from a store, not a bee tree?

17. The Five Chinese Brothers by Claire Bishop
    When one brother is to have his head cut off, the brother with the iron neck takes his place. What book is this?
    In what book does one brother take a nap inside a burning hot oven?

18. And I Mean It, Stanley by Crosby Bonsall
    In what book does a little girl tell Stanley, who is behind the fence, that she doesn't want him to even peek at what she has built?
    Name the book in which Stanley comes charging through the fence and wrecks everything the little girl has built.

19. Tell Me Some More by Crosby Bonsall
    Where can you hold an elephant under your arm?
    This book tells you. It is called....
    What book is about a special place where you can take
    home a rocket?

20. Who's a Pest? by Crosby Bonsall
    What book has four sisters named Lolly, Molly, Polly
    and Dolly, and a little brother named Homer?
    In what book does little brother Homer not only get
    his four sisters, but also a big bear, out of a deep hole?

21. Clifford the Big Red Dog by Norman Bridwell
    Emily Elizabeth has the biggest, reddest dog on the
    street. He's so big she can ride him. This very first
    book about him is called....
    Emily Elizabeth's dog is so big, he can hold a real
    car in his mouth. Name his story.

22. Georgie by Robert Bright
    When this little ghost decides to move, he finds most
    of the other houses already have ghosts in them. Name
    his story.
    What little ghost is happy to go home when he finds
    out the stairs are creaky again and the hinges on the
    door are rusty? His name is the title of the book.

23. Arthur's Eyes by Marc Brown
    Arthur accidentally walks into the girls' bathroom at
    school when he doesn't wear his glasses. Name that
    book!
    With his glasses on, Arthur makes ten baskets during
    basketball practice and he doesn't miss any math prob-
    lems at all. What is the title?

24. The Runaway Bunny by Margaret Wise Brown
    When this little bunny wants to run away, his mother
    says she will always find him. What story are they in?
    When this bunny dreams of being a bird, his mother
    says she will be a tree. Name the book.

25. Daniel's Duck by Clyde Robert Bulla
    When the people at the fair laugh at Daniel's carving,
    he grabs it and runs away. Name that book!
    Daniel doesn't want to sell the wooden duck he has

carved, but he knows what he really wants to do with it. Can you name his story?

26. Come Away from the Water, Shirley by John Burningham
     When Shirley sees a boat on the seashore, she takes an imaginary trip to a pirate ship. Name that book!
     In what book does Shirley fight pirates and walk the plank when she goes to the seashore with her parents?

27. The Very Hungry Caterpillar by Eric Carle
     What is the title of a story about a caterpillar who eats lots and lots until he gets a stomachache?
     This little caterpillar eats and eats until he is a big caterpillar, then he spins a cocoon around himself. What is the name of his story?

28. "Bee My Valentine!" by Miriam Cohen
     At the first grade's Valentine's Day party, George hides in the coatroom because he doesn't get enough valentines. What book is this?
     Name the book in which Jim uses his harmonica to cheer up George at the Valentine's Day party.

29. First Grade Takes a Test by Miriam Cohen
     In what book does the teacher explain to the first grade that a test doesn't tell important things, such as if you are kind and help your friends?
     Anna Maria is sent to a special class because she did very well on a test. What story is this?

30. The New Teacher by Miriam Cohen
     In which book do the first graders tell riddles about their new teacher on the playground before school?
     The first grade's new teacher is big and can holler loudly. What book is she in?

31. Andy and the Lion by James Daugherty
     In what book does a boy read a book about lions and then meet a real lion on his way to school?
     When Andy goes to the circus, a lion jumps out of the cage and runs straight toward him. What book is this?

32. Andy, That's My Name by Tomie De Paola
     In what book do the big kids take the letters of Andy's name and make more words with them?

Since the big kids won't let Andy play, he decides to take his name and go home. What is the title of his story?

33. <u>May I Bring a Friend?</u> by Beatrice De Regniers
This book is in rhyme and tells of an invitation to tea from a King and Queen. Can you name it?
When the King and Queen invite a boy to the castle, he always brings his animal friends with him. What book is this?

34. <u>If All the Seas Were One Sea</u> by Janina Domanska
This picture book is a nursery rhyme about all the seas and all the trees and all the axes and all the men. Can you name it?
What picture book shows a man made of all men chopping a tree made of all trees, and letting it fall into the sea?

35. <u>Drummer Hoff</u> by Barbara Emberly
This rhyming picture book shows soldiers getting a big cannon ready to fire. Do you know its name?
Captain Bammer brought the rammer and Sergeant Chowder brought the powder. What book are they in?

36. <u>One Wide River to Cross</u> by Barbara Emberly
This picture book illustrates a song about Noah's ark and shows the animals getting on the ark, one by one, two by two, three by three, and so on. Name it!
When the animals came four by four, the hippopotamus blocked the door of the ark. What is the title of this book?

37. <u>In the Forest</u> by Marie Hall Ets
With a new horn and a paper hat, a little boy leads a parade of animals through the forest. Name the book they are in.
In what book do a little boy and his animal friends go for a walk in the forest, have a picnic and play games?

38. <u>Just Me</u> by Marie Hall Ets
This little boy can't fly like a bird, but he can walk like a cat, a rooster and a cow. What book is he in?
In what book does a boy follow the animals and try to walk like they do?

39. Play with Me by Marie Hall Ets
        This little girl wants to play with a grasshopper, a
     frog, a turtle, a chipmunk, a blue jay, a rabbit and a
     snake, but they all go away. Name her story.
        When the little girl gives up on finding someone to
     play with and sits quietly, all the animals come back to
     her. What is the title of this book?

40. Where Does the Teacher Live? by Paula K. Feder
        Nancy thinks Mrs. Greengrass, her teacher, lives at
     school, but Willie says no. What book will tell you who
     is right?
        In which book do Alba, Nancy and Willie follow their
     teacher, Mrs. Greengrass, after school to see where she
     lives?

41. Harry and the Terrible Whatzit by Dick Gackenback
        Is there really something terrible down in the cellar?
     Harry goes down, armed with a broom, to save his
     mother. What book is he in?
        In what book does Harry have a fight with a two-
     headed monster in the cellar?

42. Noisy Nancy Norris by Lou Ann Gaeddert
        In what book is Nancy so noisy, she bothers everyone
     in her apartment building?
        Nancy is so noisy, that Mrs. Muffle from downstairs
     says Nancy's family will have to move. What book is
     this?

43. Fish for Supper by M.B. Goffstein
        Grandmother liked to go fishing, so she got up at
     five-o'clock in the morning in the book called....
        In what book does a grandmother catch sunfish, crap-
     pies, perch and sometimes a big northern pike?

44. Be Nice to Spiders by Margaret Graham
        Helen the spider makes the animals in the zoo happy
     by eating the flies that are bothering them. Name her
     story.
        All the spider webs are swept out of the zoo because
     the Mayor is coming to visit, but that brings back the
     flies! Name that book!

45. Ox-Cart Man by Donald Hall
        This picture book tells the story of a man who packed

his cart with all of the things his family grew and made, and travelled to Portsmouth to sell them. What is the title?

   This man sells everything he takes to Portsmouth, even his cart and ox, so he can buy a needle, a kettle, a knife and peppermint candies for his family. What picture book is he in?

46. Arthur's Honey Bear by Lillian Hoban
       In this book Arthur cannot decide whether he will sell his honey bear at his tag sale. What is the title?
       Name the book in which Violet buys her big brother's honey bear.

47. A Bargain for Frances by Russell Hoban
       By putting something in the sugar bowl, Frances tricks Thelma into taking back her tea set. Can you name the story?
       In which book do Frances and Thelma decide that being friends is better than being careful?

48. Barkley by Syd Hoff
       In which book does Barkley the dog get too old to perform in the circus?
       This book is about Barkley, an old circus dog, who runs away and is returned by some children. What is the title?

49. Danny and the Dinosaur by Syd Hoff
       When Danny goes to the museum he makes a friend-- a big dinosaur. Name his story.
       In what book does a boy take a dinosaur home to play with?

50. Rosie's Walk by Pat Hutchins
       When Rosie the hen goes for a walk in the barnyard, a fox chases her, but she doesn't even know it. Name that book!
       Which book shows a fox who starts out chasing Rosie the hen and ends up getting chased himself by a swarm of bees?

51. Willaby by Rachel Isadora
       This first grader would rather draw than do anything else, especially lessons--and that gets her in trouble with Miss Finney. Name her story.

When this first grader runs out of paper to draw on, she uses the walls and her desk. Her name is the title of the book. What is it?

52. <u>Three Jovial Huntsmen</u> by Susan Jeffers
    The three huntsmen in this book can't find anything to hunt, but the reader can see lots of animals on the pages. What is the title of this book?
    The huntsmen couldn't agree whether what they found was a hedgehog or a pincushion with the pins stuck in the wrong way. Name that book!

53. <u>Peter's Chair</u> by Ezra Jack Keats
    When Peter finds out his parents want to paint his chair pink for the new baby, he decides to run away. What is the title of this story?
    In this book Peter and his dog Willie run away from home to rescue Peter's little chair from a paintbrush. Can you give the title?

54. <u>The Snowy Day</u> by Ezra Jack Keats
    When Peter wakes up, he looks out his window and sees lots and lots of snow, so he goes out and makes a snowman and angels and slides down a snow mountain. What is the name of his story?
    In this book Peter dreams that the sun melts all the snow, but when he wakes up he is happy to see new snow falling outside his window. What is the title?

55. <u>Whose Mouse Are You?</u> by Robert Kraus
    This little mouse saves his mother from the cat, frees his father from a trap and goes after his sister in a hot air balloon. Name his story.
    What picture book shows a little mouse who has no family with him until he rescues them from the cat, the trap and a far-off mountain?

56. <u>Frog Went A-Courtin'</u> by John Langstaff
    In what book do a frog and a mouse get married and have a wedding breakfast of three green beans and a black-eyed pea?
    Can you name the book that has a wedding party attended by ants, a goose, a bumblebee, a coon, a snake, a moth, a fly, and a chick?

57. <u>Finders Keepers</u> by William Lipkind and Nicholas Mordvinoff
    Name the book in which Winkle and Nap, two dogs, argue over a bone?
    What book has Winkle and Nap, two dogs who get very strange haircuts from Mr. Hairtrimmer?

58. <u>Frog and Toad Are Friends</u> by Arnold Lobel
    This book has five stories in it. One is about Toad standing on his head so he can think of a story to tell Frog, who is sick in bed. What is the title of the book?
    In one story of this book, Frog and Toad find lots and lots of buttons, but none of them are the one Toad lost. Name that book!

59. <u>Frog and Toad Together</u> by Arnold Lobel
    When Toad writes a list of things to do, it works fine until the list blows away. Name that book!
    In what book do birds get to eat a whole box of chocolate chip cookies so two friends can get some will power?

60. <u>There's a Nightmare in My Closet</u> by Mercer Mayer
    This boy puts on his army helmet, gets his popgun and frightens the monster that comes out of his closet. What book is he in?
    In which picture book does a nightmare cry after getting shot with a popgun?

61. <u>Blueberries for Sal</u> by Robert McCloskey
    When this little girl goes with her mother to pick blueberries, she ends up following a bear! Name that book!
    This little girl eats more blueberries on Blueberry Hill than she puts in her pail. What is the title of her story?

62. <u>Make Way for Ducklings</u> by Robert McCloskey
    In this book Mr. and Mrs. Mallard find a perfect place to raise their family in Boston. Can you name the book?
    Jack, Kack, Lack, Mack, Nack, Oack, Pack and Quack are characters in this story set in Boston. What is the title?

63. <u>Little Bear's Visit</u> by Else Minarek
    In which book does Grandmother tell Little Bear about the time his mother found a baby robin?

While Little Bear runs to bring Grandfather Bear his
pipe, Grandfather goes to sleep. What book are they in?

64. Cinderella by Charles Perrault
Name the fairytale in which a fairy godmother helps a
poor step-daughter attend the ball.
She has two ugly step-sisters who boss her around
all the time. Her name is the title of the book. It is....

65. Peter and the Wolf by Sergei Prokofiev
What story tells how Peter catches the wolf that has
swallowed his friend, the duck?
Grandfather warns his grandson of the dangers of the
meadow, and his fears come true when a wolf comes out of
of the forest and eats the duck. What book is this?

66. Spectacles by Ellen Raskin
When Iris Fogel sees a chestnut mare in the parlor
instead of her baby sitter, her mother knows she needs
glasses! What book is she in?
Iris Fogel's mother chooses eye glass frames for Iris
that make her look smart instead of cute because Iris
needs to impress her teacher in this book called....

67. Curious George by H.A. Rey
Name the little monkey who is captured in the jungle
by a man in a big yellow hat. Then you will have the
title of the book!
What book tells about a monkey who calls the fire
station and ends up in prison?

68. In the Night Kitchen by Maurice Sendak
In what picture book does a noise wake up Mickey,
who then falls through the dark, out of his pajamas, and
into the kitchen?
In this book Mickey gets made into a Mickey-Cake by
three fat bakers. Name it!

69. Where the Wild Things Are by Maurice Sendak
When Max threatens to eat his mother up, he is sent
to bed with no supper. Can you name his story?
In which story does a forest grow right in Max's bed-
room?

70. The Cat in the Hat by Dr. Seuss

In what book does a goldfish warn Sally and her brother not to play with a strange looking cat who shows up on a rainy day?

In what book will you find kites flying in the house, a fish in a teapot, rakes, umbrellas, balls and birthday cakes all over the floor--all because of a cat?

71. Gregory the Terrible Eater by Mitchell Sharmat
Gregory and his parents can't agree on what is good food. He likes fruit and vegetables. His parents like shoes and tires! Name that book!

Dr. Ram tells Gregory's parents to give Gregory one new food each day as a cure for his peculiar illness-- eating human food instead of goat food. What book is this?

72. Caps for Sale by Esphyr Slobodkina
In this book a cap peddler goes to sleep under a tree and loses all the caps he was selling. Can you give the title?

In this book the monkeys in the tree imitate every- thing the peddler does, and that's how he gets his stolen caps back. Name that book!

73. Rain Drop Splash by Alvin Tresselt
This picture book starts with the rain falling, and shows how it ends up in a river flowing to the sea. Can you name it?

It rains so long, the water covers the road and the children have to go to school in a boat. What picture book is this?

74. White Snow, Bright Snow by Alvin Tresselt
This picture book shows the postman, the farmer and the policeman getting ready for the snow. Can you name it?

What book shows snow falling and covering the town while the farmer milks his cow and the policeman stays home in bed?

75. A Tree Is Nice by Janice May Udry
What book shows us that trees are good for climbing and giving us fruit and hanging swings in and many more things?

What book shows us that trees are good for giving shade for cows and people and keeping houses cool?

76. The Biggest Bear by Lynd Ward
    Every barn in the valley has a bearskin on it except
    Johnny's. In what book does he set out to shoot a bear
    in order to get a bearskin?
    Johnny sets out to shoot a bear and ends up feeding
    one maple sugar instead. Name that book!

77. Umbrella by Taro Yashima
    In what book is Momo very very happy because it is
    raining and she can finally use her birthday presents?
    The first day that Momo used her umbrella was also
    the first day she didn't hold her mother or father's hand.
    Name her story.

78. Louis the Fish by Arthur Yorinks
    Louis, a butcher, is not happy because he hates meat.
    He's always hated meat. What book is he in?
    Louis, surrounded by steaks all day, can only think
    about fish in this book called....

79. Harry the Dirty Dog by Gene Zion
    This white dog with black spots plays in so much dirt
    he becomes a black dog with white spots. Name his
    story!
    In what book does a white dog with black spots be-
    come so dirty his family doesn't know him?

80. Mr. Rabbit and the Lovely Present by Charlotte Zolotow
    In what book does a little girl ask a rabbit for help
    in finding a birthday present for her mother?
    A basket of fruit makes a good birthday present, de-
    cides the little girl, so she thanks Mr. Rabbit. Name
    that book!

                    ADVANCED READING

81. Who's in Rabbit's House? by Verna Aardema
    In what book does a mysterious animal called The
    Long One not let Rabbit get into her own house?
    Name the book in which a frog pretends to be a spit-
    ting cobra so he can scare someone out of Rabbit's house.

82. Why Mosquitos Buzz in People's Ears by Verna Aardema
    When a mosquito tells a story to an iguana, it starts

bad feelings that eventually result in the death of a baby
owl. What book is this?
In what book does an iguana put sticks in his ears so
he won't have to listen to a mosquito's lies?

83. The Great Valentine's Day Balloon Race by Adrienne
Adams
In what book is a hot air balloon named Bonnie's Val-
entine?
Name the book in which a rabbit family builds a hot
air balloon so Orson can race.

84. Black Is Brown Is Tan by Arnold Adoff
What book tells about a family in which the daddy is
white, the mom, black, and the children, brown?
In what book does the daddy's face get tomato red
when he sends the children to bed?

85. Miss Nelson Is Missing by Harry Allard
What book is about the kids in Room 207 and their
very unusual substitute teacher?
Name the book in which the worst behaved class in
the whole school asks the police to find their teacher.

86. Thumbelina by Hans Christian Andersen
This little girl was born from a flower that grew from
a barleycorn. Her name is the title of the story. Do
you know it?
In what story is a tiny girl who sleeps in a walnut
shell kidnapped by a toad to be a wife for his son?

87. Humbug Witch by Lorna Balian
This witch is very small and has a black cat named
Fred. Her name is the title of the book. What is it?
This little witch gets very tired of being a witch, so
she takes off her apron, shawl, shoes, hat, gloves and
long stringy red hair, and goes to bed! Name her story.

88. Wiley and the Hairy Man by Molly Bang
This boy tricks the Hairy Man into changing himself
into a possum, then puts him in a bag and throws him
in the river. Can you name the story?
If Wiley can fool the monster just one more time, it
will never come back again. Name that book!

89. <u>Peter Pan</u> by J.M. Barrie
    Name the book in which three English children have
a Newfoundland dog for a nurse.
    What boy ran away from home the day he was born?
His name is the name of the book.

90. <u>Jack-O'-Lantern</u> by Edna Barth
    This story is about the very first jack-o'-lantern and
a very mean blacksmith. Can you name it?
    Name the book in which Mean Jack the blacksmith
tricks the Devil's sons, so the Devil himself comes to
get him.

91. <u>Hawk, I'm Your Brother</u> by Byrd Baylor
    Rudy thinks that if he steals a hawk from Santos
Mountain, he will learn to fly. Name that book!
    In what book does an Indian boy climb a steep moun-
tain to capture a young hawk?

92. <u>The Sun Is a Golden Earring</u> by Natalia Belting
    This book says that the Chippewa Indians believed
that great birds flapped their wings, which were clouds,
to make winds. Can you name it?
    Name the book that shows men's first ideas about
nature. One was that the stars are a woman's necklace.

93. <u>Madeline</u> by Ludwig Bemelmans
    This is the first book written about a little girl who
lives with eleven other little girls in an old house in
Paris. Can you give the title?
    Madeline is proud to show her eleven friends the scar
from her operation. Can you name the book?

94. <u>Madeline's Rescue</u> by Ludwig Bemelmans
    In which book does Madeline fall off a bridge into the
river in Paris?
    Name the book in which Madeline is rescued from
drowning by a white dog named Miss Genevieve.

95. <u>The Terrible Thing That Happened at Our House</u> by
Marge Blaine
    Things are pretty bad at her house after her mother
goes back to work, until this little girl starts yelling.
Name that book!
    Dressing herself, making her bed and eating lunch in

the school cafeteria are a few of the things the little
girl in this book must start doing, because her mother
has gone back to work. What book is she in?

96. The One in the Middle Is the Green Kangaroo by Judy
     Blume
         Freddy Dissel thinks it's no fun being the middle
     child ... until he gets a part in the school play. What
     is the title of this book?
         In which book does Freddy get a part in the school
     play because he is a good jumper and can talk loudly?

97. Arthur's Valentine by Marc Brown
         Who is Arthur's Secret Admirer who keeps sending
     him valentines? Can you name this mystery?
         When Arthur's secret valentines fall out of his pocket,
     he gets teased by his friends. Name that book!

98. Once a Mouse by Marcia Brown
         In order to save a little mouse from danger, a hermit
     changes it into bigger and bigger animals. What is the
     name of this story?
         When the mouse is changed into a tiger, he becomes
     so proud he gets a scolding. Tell which book he is in.

99. Stone Soup by Marcia Brown
         Three clever soldiers make a wonderful soup with
     only three smooth stones. What book is this?
         As the soldiers stir their magic soup, the villagers
     remember that they have a few things to add, such as
     cabbage, carrots and meat. What book are they in?

100. Wheel on the Chimney by Margaret Wise Brown
         This book tells of how the storks fly from the North
     to Africa, where it is warm, to spend the winter. Can
     you name it?
         In this book farmers tie wheels on their chimneys so
     the storks will have a place to make their nests. Name
     that book!

101. The Story of Babar by Jean De Brunhoff
         This little elephant is happy until a hunter kills his
     mother. Name that book!
         A rich old lady gives an elephant money, clothes,
     fine food, lessons and even a car! What book is she in?

102. <u>Katy and the Big Snow</u> by Virginia Burton
       Katy is a big red crawler tractor. What is the name
of her story?
       When the city of Geoppolis is covered by snow, only
Katy with her snow plow can get through. What book
is she in?

103. <u>The Little House</u> by Virginia Burton
       This house, built out in the country, watches as a
city grows all around her. What is her story called?
       Name the book in which the great-great-granddaughter
of the man who built this sad house knows just what to
do to make it happy.

104. <u>Mike Mulligan and His Steam Shovel</u> by Virginia Burton
       This picture book is about a man with a big red
steam shovel named Mary Anne. Can you name it?
       Mary Anne, the steam shovel, has helped build many
wonderful things, but now there are more modern machines to take her place and she is very sad. What
book is this?

105. <u>Go and Hush the Baby</u> by Betsy Byars
       Will is all ready to play baseball, but the baby is
crying, so Will has to stay and make him happy. Can
you name this book?
       In what book is the baby happy while Will tells a
story or tickles him, but cries everytime Will tries to
leave?

106. <u>The Accident</u> by Carol Carrick
       Christopher's dog, Bodger, waited too long to cross
the road; by that time the truck was too close! Name
this book.
       Christopher thought his father would make everything
alright after his dog, Bodger, is hit by a truck. Can
you name this book?

107. <u>Alice's Adventures in Wonderland</u> by Lewis Carroll
       This little girl is afraid of drowning in a pool of her
own tears, and when she eats a cake, she grows nine
feet tall! What is the title of her story?
       The Queen's way of solving any problem is to behead
someone, and Alice is afraid she is next. What is the
title of this classic?

108. Spooky Night by Natalie Savage Carson
     Spooky, the Bascomb's cat, doesn't like it when Hal-
     loween comes and the Bascomb girl dresses in a witch
     costume. Name that book!
     Spooky can stay with the Bascomb family if he can
     catch the moon for his witch mistress, in this book
     called....

109. Chanticleer and the Fox by Geoffrey Chaucer
     When Chanticleer closes his eyes and begins to crow,
     he is grabbed by the throat and carried off toward the
     woods. Name that book!
     Which book shows a poor widow, her two daughters
     and all the farm animals chasing a fox who carries a
     rooster in his mouth?

110. The Carp in the Bathtub by Barbara Cohen
     Leah and Harry don't have to take a bath all week
     because a big fish is living in the bathtub. Name that
     book!
     Leah and Harry's mother makes the best gefilte fish
     in New York City, but Leah and Harry won't eat it be-
     cause its main ingredient is a good friend of theirs.
     What is the name of this book?

111. Molly's Pilgrim by Barbara Cohen
     In what book does Molly, a third grader who is also
     a Russian emigrant, learn about the first Thanksgiving?
     Name the book in which Molly is ashamed to show
     her classmates the doll her mother made for a class as-
     signment on Thanksgiving.

112. The Adventures of Pinocchio by Carlo Collodi
     In what book does old Geppetto make a marionette
     that can dance, fence and even turn somersaults?
     When this boy-puppet tells a lie, his nose grows
     longer and longer. What book is he in?

113. Impossible Possum by Ellen Conford
     What book tells about Randolph, who can't sleep up-
     side down like other possums?
     Randolph Possum keeps getting a headache from fall-
     ing on his head, until he discovers tree sap. What book
     is he in?

114. Clyde Monster by Robert L. Crowe
        Can you name the little monster who doesn't want to
      go to bed in his cave because he is afraid of the dark?
      His name is the title of the book.
        Clyde is not afraid of monsters. He is afraid of peo-
      ple. What is the title of his story?

115. Abraham Lincoln by Ingri and Edgar D'Aulaire
        This Caldecott Award Winner tells us the true story
      of our sixteenth President. What is the title?
        Which Caldecott Award Winner tells of a boy born in
      a little log cabin in Kentucky who became President and
      held the nation together through the Civil War?

116. Big Anthony and the Magic Ring by Tomie De Paola
        Name the book in which Big Anthony becomes so
      handsome that all the women in the village chase after
      him.
        Strega Nona's magic ring makes Big Anthony too
      handsome for the village women to resist, in this book
      called....

117. The Clown of God by Tomie De Paola
        When old Giovanni drops the balls he is juggling,
      the people throw stones and vegetables at him. What
      book is he in?
        The old man's present for the Lady and her Holy
      Child is to juggle for them. Then when he falls on the
      floor, something amazing happens. Name that book!

118. Helga's Dowry; A Troll Love Story by Tomie De Paola
        Unmarried troll maidens must wander the earth for-
      ever, but trolls can't marry without a dowry and Helga
      doesn't have one, in this book called....
        In what book does Helga, a troll, wash laundry,
      make people young and beautiful again, and chop down
      trees to earn a dowry so she can marry?

119. The Legend of the Bluebonnet; An Old Tale of Texas
      by Tomie De Paola
        Name the book in which She-Who-Is-Alone gives her
      most valued possession to the Great Spirits.
        In this book a Comanche Indian girl's name is changed
      from She-Who-Is-Alone to One-Who-Dearly-Loved-Her-
      People. What is its title?

120. Nana Upstairs and Nana Downstairs by Tomie De Paola
        Every Sunday Tommy visited his grandparents and
his great-grandmother who stayed upstairs in bed.
What is the name of his story?
        Tommy's older brother thinks their great-grandmother
looks like a witch when she lets her hair down, but
Tommy thinks she's beautiful. Can you name this book?

121. The Quicksand Book by Tomie De Paola
        When Jungle Girl falls into quicksand, Jungle Boy
comes to the rescue--with a lot of facts. Name that
book!
        What book tells you how you can make your own
quicksand?

122. Strega Nona: An Old Tale Retold by Tomie De Paola
        In what book does an old witch hire Big Anthony to
take care of her house and garden, but tells him never
to touch the pasta pot?
        What book shows a witch's house overflowing with so
much pasta that it runs out the doors and windows and
down the street?

123. Strega Nona's Magic Lessons by Tomie De Paola
        In this book, Bambolona, the baker's daughter, has
too much work, so she goes to Strega Nona for help.
What is its title?
        If Bambolona is going to learn Strega Nona's magic,
Big Anthony wants to learn it too, but he can't because he isn't a strega. What book is he in?

124. Liang and the Magic Paintbrush by Demi
        What book has a boy with a special paintbrush that
makes whatever he paints come to life?
        The special brush won't work for the greedy emperor;
it only works for Liang. Name that book.

125. Old Black Witch by Wende Devlin
        When Nicky and his mother open The Jug and Muffin
tea room, it's a big success, even though it's supposed
to be haunted! Name that book!
        Name the book in which two thieves are turned into
toads and kept in a witch's room above The Jug and
Muffin tea shop.

126. Cranberry Christmas by Wende and Harry Devlin
        In which book does old Cyrus Grape chase Mr. Whis-
      kers and the children off of the pond?
        Name the book in which Maggie and Grandmother
      decorate Mr. Whisker's Christmas tree with sea shells.

127. Cranberry Thanksgiving by Wende and Harry Devlin
        Grandmother is not happy that Maggie has invited
      Mr. Whiskers to Thanksgiving dinner, because she is
      afraid he will steal her secret recipe. Name that book!
        Just because a man smells good and has a gold cane
      doesn't mean you should trust him. In what book does
      Mr. Whiskers teach Grandmother this lesson?

128. Petunia by Roger Duvoisin
        This silly goose finds a book and becomes very
      proud. Her name is the name of this book. What is it?
        First Petunia the goose finds a book and thinks she's
      wise. Then she finds a box and discovers that she is
      not wise at all. What is the title?

129. Nine Days to Christmas by Marie Hall Ets and Aurora
      Labastida
        Christmas in Mexico is what this book is about, and
      Ceci's very special piñata. What is the title?
        Ceci chooses the most beautiful piñata in the world
      for her Christmas posada. But she doesn't remember
      that piñatas are made to be broken. Name her story.

130. The Happy Lion by Louise Fatio
        This lion lives in a house in a zoo in France. His
      name is the title of the book. What is it?
        When this friendly lion goes out on the street for a
      walk, he cannot understand why people are not as po-
      lite as they are when they visit him in the zoo. Name
      his story.

131. Jambo Means Hello by Muriel Feelings
        This book has pictures from East Africa and teaches
      us one word of Swahili for each letter of the alphabet.
      Can you name it?
        In Swahili, Baba means father and Mama means mother.
      Those are only two of the words you can learn in this
      alphabet book called....

132. Moja Means One by Muriel Feelings
     This is a counting book in Swahili, the language of
     East Africa. Can you name it?
     This book shows you scenes from East Africa as it
     teaches you to count in Swahili. Name that book!

133. Prayer for a Child by Rachel Field
     Can you name the book which is a prayer written
     for a little girl?
     What Caldecott Award Winner tells a little girl's bed-
     time prayer?

134. Walter the Lazy Mouse by Marjorie Flack
     In this book a young mouse is so lazy that his fam-
     ily forgets all about him and moves away. Can you give
     the title?
     Name the book in which a little mouse named Walter
     lives on Mouse Island with the three frogs, Lulu, Lean-
     der and Percy.

135. A Pocket for Corduroy by Don Freeman
     This little toy bear searches in a laundromat for a
     pocket for himself. Can you name his story?
     Corduroy the bear thinks he is sliding down a snowy
     mountain, but it is really soap flakes. What is the title
     of this book?

136. George Washington's Breakfast by Jean Fritz
     George's grandmother has promised to cook him a
     breakfast just like President Washington's--if he can
     find out what it was. Name that book!
     Name the book in which George Allen finds an old
     book in the attic called THE AMERICAN ORACLE, which
     has the answer to his question about President Washing-
     ton.

137. Millions of Cats by Wanda Gag
     When the very old man asks the cats which one is
     prettiest, they begin to fight and quarrel until they eat
     one another all up. What book is this?
     The old man finds so many cats that they drink up
     a whole pond. Name that book!

138. Mrs. Gaddy and the Ghost by Wilson Gage
     In which book does a farmer try to get rid of a

ghost with a broom, bug spray, a fire, a mousetrap
and finally a letter?
    Name the book in which a ghost cries over a letter
sending him away?

139. King of the Cats by Paul Galdone
          In this book a gravedigger tells his wife and cat
      about nine black cats carrying a coffin. What is the
      title?
          The gravedigger brings an important message to
      Tom Tildrum from nine black cats. Name this spooky
      book!

140. Rotten Ralph by Jack Gantos
          Sarah's family is so angry with Ralph, her cat, that
      they leave him at the circus. What book is this?
          What very naughty cat has to sweep up popcorn and
      water the camels at the circus? His name is the title
      of the book.

141. Fair's Fair by Leon Garfield
          Jackson finds a key attached to the collar of a big,
      black dog. They set off together to find a door the
      key will fit in this book called....
          Jackson and Lillipolly are led to the big house by a
      black dog. Once there, they're well cared for, but they
      never see their caretaker. Name that book!

142. Today Was a Terrible Day by Patricia Reilly Giff
          Name the book in which Ronald accidentally eats
      Jimmy's lunch at school.
          After Ronald Morgan has a very bad day in second
      grade, his teacher sends a surprising note home. What
      book is this?

143. The Gift of the Sacred Dog by Paul Goble
          The hungry Indian people travel in search of buffalo
      but find none until the Great Spirit sends them a gift.
      Name that book!
          What book tells the legend of how horses first came
      to the Indian people?

144. The Girl Who Loved Wild Horses by Paul Goble
          This book tells of an Indian girl who loves horses so
      much, she goes to live with them. What is its title?

In this beautiful book an Indian girl lives with the wild horses but brings her parents a colt each year. Can you name the book?

145. The Bremen Town Musicians by The Brothers Grimm
This tale is about a strange musical group made up of a donkey, a dog, a cat and a rooster, who scare robbers out of a house. What is the title?
These four animals are on their way to Bremen to become musicians, until they find a house full of robbers. Name that book!

146. Briar Rose/Sleeping Beauty by The Brothers Grimm
In what tale does an evil fairy warn the king and queen that their daughter will prick her finger on a spinning wheel and die when she is fifteen?
Everyone in the kingdom falls asleep for years and years in this story. Can you name it?

147. Rapunzel by The Brothers Grimm
This beautiful girl with long golden hair was named after a kind of lettuce. In what book is she shut up in a tower by a wicked witch?
In this fairy tale, a prince hears beautiful singing coming from the top of a tower. There he discovers a girl with long, golden hair. Can you give the title?

148. The Big Snow by Berta and Elmer Hader
The old man and the old woman in the little stone house saved the forest animals in this book by putting food out in the snow. What is its name?
The raccoons and skunks were all ready for winter, but the birds, deer and rabbits were happy when the little old woman, dressed in green, scattered food on the snow. Name that book!

149. A Story, A Story by Gail Haley
The Sky God's price for selling his stories to Ananse is a leopard, a hornet and a fairy. What African folktale is this?
This book tells how Ananse buys the Sky God's stories and spreads them to all the corners of the world. What is its title?

150. Mei Li by Thomas Handforth
This girl follows San Yu to the New Year Fair even

though little girls are supposed to stay home. Her name
is the title of the book. What is it?

If this little girl doesn't pass through the city gate
before it closes, she'll not get home to greet the Kitchen
God on the New Year. What book is she in?

151. Tight Times by Barbara Shook Hazen
His family is too poor to let the boy have a dog, but
he does get to keep the kitten he finds in a garbage
can. Can you name that book?

This boy wants a dog to eat food that he doesn't
like, but instead he gets a cat. What book is he in?

152. The Shrinking of Treehorn by Florence Parry Heide
In what book does Treehorn grow so small that he
can walk under his bed?

Name the book where a boy keeps shrinking until he
finds a game to help himself grow bigger.

153. The Country Bunny and the Little Gold Shoes by Du
Bose Heyward
This book tells us that there are really five Easter
Bunnies who work for Grandfather Bunny. Can you
name it?

In which book does the Cottontail Easter Bunny have
to carry a very special egg to a sick boy on the top of
an icy mountain?

154. Moonsong Lullaby by Jamake Highwater
At night the Moon sings to her husband, the mighty
golden Sun, who is sleeping. Name that book.

Even though the Indians sleep, the Moon keeps singing all through the night in this book called....

155. Evan's Corner by Elizabeth Hill
At last Evan has found a place of his very own in
his large family's small flat. He even paints a picture
at school to hang there. What book is he in?

There are eight corners in the apartment, so each
member of Evan's family can have one, says Evan's
mother. What book is this?

156. Emmet Otter's Jug-Band Christmas by Russell Hoban
Emmet Otter wants to buy Ma a piano for Christmas
and Ma Otter wants to buy him a guitar, but they are
too poor. Name their story.

In which book does Emmet take his mother's washtub and broom to enter a talent show so he can buy her a piano with the prize money?

157. The Contest by Nonny Hogrogian
     In this story Ehleezah is engaged to two robbers at the same time but they don't know it. What is the title? When Hrahad and Hmayag discover that they are both clever robbers, they decide that Ehleezah doesn't deserve either one of them. Name this book.

158. One Fine Day by Nonny Hogrogian
     When a thirsty fox drinks the old woman's milk, she chops off his tail. What is the title of this book? If the fox brings grass for the cow, the cow will give him milk for the old woman, who will then give the fox his tail back. Name that book!

159. David and Dog by Shirley Hughes
     When David goes for a walk with his family, he loses his favorite stuffed toy and has a hard time sleeping without it. What is the title of the story? In what book does David finally find his favorite stuffed animal, only to discover that it has been sold to someone else at the Summer Fair?

160. George the Babysitter by Shirley Hughes
     This book is about a babysitter who takes care of Mike, Jenny and Baby Sue while their mother works in the afternoons. What is the title? In what book do Mike and Jenny give Baby Sue a bath while the babysitter washes the dishes?

161. Mystery on the Docks by Thatcher Hurd
     Ralph and Eduardo have been kidnapped so Eduardo sings for help. Can you name this book? In what book will you meet Ralph, who is a short-order cook at his diner on Pier 46?

162. Ben's Trumpet by Rachel Isadora
     What book tells about a boy who sits on the fire escape playing an imaginary trumpet each night? Ben longs to play jazz, but he has no instrument ... until the trumpeter from the Zig Zag Jazz Club helps him out. Name his story.

163. Max by Rachel Isadora
        What book has a boy who plays baseball every Sat-
      urday but only after he goes to his sister's dance class?
        Stretches at the barre, splits and leaps are exercises
      a boy uses to help him warm up for baseball games.
      He learned them at his sister's dance class. Can you
      name this book?

164. Goggles by Ezra Jack Keats
        Name the book in which Peter gets knocked down
      by two big boys because they want the motorcycle gog-
      gles he has found?
        Archie, Peter and Willie hide from the big boys in
      their hideout, then run for home with their new yellow
      goggles. Name that book!

165. A Letter to Amy by Ezra Jack Keats
        Peter especially wants Amy to come to his birthday
      party, so he writes her a letter. This book is called....
        In this book Amy arrives at Peter's birthday party
      with a parrot in a cage. What is the title?

166. Can I Keep Him? by Steven Kellogg
        Every time Arnold brings an animal home, his mother
      finds many reasons not to keep it ... until Arnold fi-
      nally finds Ralph. Name his story.
        Dogs are too noisy, and Arnold's grandma is allergic
      to cat fur. In what book does Arnold dream of bring-
      ing home deer, bears, tigers, pythons and dinosaurs?

167. The Island of the Skog by Steven Kellogg
        Before they leave their ship, the Rowdies fire twelve
      cannonballs to show the Skog who is boss. What book
      are they in?
        When the Skog walks into the Rowdies' trap, it's
      pulled into the sky and falls apart! Name that book!

168. The Mysterious Tadpole by Steven Kellogg
        Louis' Uncle McAllister sends him a tadpole from
      Scotland who eats several cheeseburgers everyday.
      Name that book!
        When Mrs. Shelbert sees six children riding on Al-
      phonse, she decides he is not an ordinary tadpole.
      What is the title?

169. <u>Ralph's Secret Weapon</u> by Steven Kellogg
     In what book does Aunt Georgiana want Ralph to
     charm a sea serpent by playing his bassoon?
     Ralph's aunt bakes him a banana-spinach cream cake
     but he decides not to eat it in this book called....

170. <u>Fat Cat</u> by Jack Kent
     In what book does a cat eat a pot of gruel and the
     pot too?
     This cat eats everything he sees, even people!
     Name that book!

171. <u>The Elephant's Child</u> by Rudyard Kipling
     This story tells how the elephant ended up with a
     long trunk--all because of curiosity and a crocodile.
     Can you name it?
     On the banks of the great grey-green, greasy Lim-
     popo River, the little elephant finds out exactly what
     the crocodile has for dinner! Name that book!

172. <u>The Man Who Tried to Save Time</u> by Phyllis Krasilovsky
     This man wants to save time, so he eats his break-
     fast at dinner time and dresses for work before he goes
     to bed! Name that book!
     In order to save time, this man eats his orange juice,
     eggs, toast and coffee all together in one bowl. What
     is the title?

173. <u>One Tough Turkey; a Thanksgiving Story</u> by Steven
     Kroll
     In what book does Solomon dump turkey feathers all
     over a group of Pilgrims?
     According to this book, the Pilgrims ate squash, not
     turkey, for their Thanksgiving dinner. Can you name
     it?

174. <u>Santa's Crash-Bang Christmas</u> by Steven Kroll
     Santa starts out falling from his sleigh on the Syl-
     vesters' roof. And from there, things get worse! What
     book is this?
     In what book does Santa chase a polar bear upstairs
     and out the window at the Sylvesters' house?

175. <u>They Were Strong and Good</u> by Robert Lawson
     In this true book the author's father fought in the

Civil War and rode a mule named Epaminondas. What
is the title?
This biography shows how the author's grandmother
spent much of her honeymoon trip being seasick on the
ship Eliza Jane Hopper. Can you name it?

176. Always Room for One More by Sorche Nic Leodhas
There were so many people in Lachie MacLachlan's
house, that it finally dinged down! What book is this?
Lachie MacLachlan had a wife and ten children but
they welcomed everyone into their little house. Name
their story.

177. Wacky Wednesday by Theo LeSieg
Everywhere he goes, this boy finds more and more
crazy things, like trees growing out of chimneys. Name
his story.
When the boy counts twenty more wacky things, he
can finally go to bed. What is the name of this picture
book?

178. Alexander and the Wind-Up Mouse by Leo Lionni
Name the book in which a real mouse and a toy mouse
become good friends.
Alexander the mouse is tired of being chased by the
broom. He wants to be like Willy so he will be loved.
Name his story.

179. Frederick by Leo Lionni
All the little mice are busy storing corn, nuts, wheat
and straw for winter--all but one. He is gathering sun
rays, colors and words. Name his story.
Even though this little mouse is not working like the
other mice to get ready for winter, he is not really
lazy; he is a poet. His name is the title of the book.
What is it?

180. Inch by Inch by Leo Lionni
Name the book in which an inchworm saves himself
from being eaten by proving how useful he is to measure
things.
If the inchworm can't measure a nightingale's song,
he'll get eaten for breakfast! Name his story.

181. Fables by Arnold Lobel

One story in this collection is about a wolf who dresses up as an apple tree to catch a hen. Name that book!

In "The Camel Dances," one story in this book, a camel wants to become a ballet dancer. Can you give the book's title?

182. The Giant Jam Sandwich by John Lord
Bap the Baker knows how to get rid of all the wasps in Itching Down. Name that book!

In what book do the townspeople make a special picnic lunch for four million wasps?

183. Through Grandpa's Eyes by Patricia MacLachlan
Because Grandpa is blind, he sees things differently than other people. In what book does he teach John to see with his fingers and ears and nose?

Name the book in which John and his blind grandfather play their cellos together.

184. Three by the Sea by Edward Marshall
In what book do three friends tell each other stories? Spider's story is the best of all because it scares his friends.

Spider tells Lolly and Sam a story about a monster who doesn't eat rats, cheese or cats but he does eat children! Name that book!

185. George and Martha by James Marshall
George hates split pea soup, so he pours it into his loafers. What book is he in?

When George breaks off his favorite tooth, the dentist replaces it with a gold one in this book called....

186. Yummers! by James Marshall
When Emily Pig goes for a walk with Eugene Turtle to lose weight, she finds lots of good snacks, in this book called....

Sandwiches, corn-on-the-cob, scones, Eskimo pies, Girl Scout cookies and lots more are all part of Emily Pig's walk, which she takes to lose weight! Can you name this book?

187. Chameleon Was a Spy by Diane Massie
Name the book in which a chameleon applies for a super secret job.

In what book does the Pleasant Pickle Company hire
a spy to get their secret formula back from the Perfect
Pickle Company?

188. One Morning in Maine by Robert McCloskey
      This picture book tells about Sal going to Buck's
Harbor with her father. Can you name it?
      When Sal gets her first loose tooth, she tells the
fish hawk, the loon, and the seal, then she falls in the
water! Name that book!

189. Arrow to the Sun; A Pueblo Indian Tale by Gerald
McDermott
      What Pueblo Indian folktale tells about the Boy who
leaves home to find his father, the Lord of the Sun?
      In what book does a Pueblo Indian boy turn into an
arrow and fly all the way to the sun?

190. The Egg Tree by Katherine Milhous
      This book tells of an Easter Egg Hunt and six painted
eggs found in a beaver hat. What is the title?
      It's as pretty as a Christmas tree, but it's for Easter,
so it has eggs hanging on it. What book is it in?

191. Winnie the Pooh by A.A. Milne
      In which book does a little bear roll in the mud until
he is black all over, then float up in the air holding a
blue balloon?
      This little bear eats so much honey, he gets stuck
trying to get out of Rabbit's hole. What book is he in?

192. One Zillion Valentines by Frank Modell
      What book tells of Marvin's and Milton's great idea
for Valentine's Day?
      Name the book in which Marvin and Milton make val-
entines for everyone in their neighborhood.

193. The Funny Little Woman by Arlene Mosel
      This book tells of a Japanese woman who follows her
rice dumpling under the ground into the home of the
wicked oni. Name that book!
      With only one grain of rice, you can soon have a
potful ... if you have the magic paddle. What book is
it in?

194. Rosie's Birthday Present by Marietta Moskin
     Carlos, Maria and Manuel all have a birthday present
     for Mamma, but their not quite five-year-old sister has
     none. What book are they in?
     A button, a pen, a key ring, a bag of party favors,
     ice cream sandwiches and a cracked mirror all help get
     Mamma a birthday present in this book called....

195. Ashanti to Zulu by Margaret Musgrove
     This picture book shows twenty-six different tribes
     of Africa, one for each letter of the alphabet. Can you
     name it?
     Each letter of the alphabet stands for an African
     tribe, in this book called....

196. Sam, Bangs and Moonshine by Evaline Ness
     When Samantha sends Thomas to Blue Rock to look
     for her pet kangaroo, she doesn't think of the danger
     until it is too late. What is the title?
     In what book does Bangs the cat get washed away by
     the tide?

197. Marshmallow by Clare Newberry
     What story tells of a baby bunny who moves in with
     Oliver the cat and Miss Tilly?
     In this book Oliver the cat opens the door and gets
     in where the baby bunny is kept. What is the title?

198. The Day Jimmy's Boa Ate the Wash by Trinka Hakes
     Noble
     When Jimmy brings his pet snake on a class field
     trip to a farm, he finds out that chickens don't like
     snakes. What book is this?
     Jimmy takes his pet snake on a class field trip to
     a farm, but he returns from the trip with a different
     pet. Name that book.

199. Suho and the White Horse by Yuzo Otsuka
     Instead of giving Suho the prize for winning the
     race, the governor beats Suho and steals his horse in
     this book called....
     Even though the horse has many arrows in its flanks,
     it still runs and runs to get back to Suho. Name that
     book!

200. <u>Amelia Bedelia</u> by Peggy Parish
        This maid thinks "dust the furniture," means she
      should put dust on the furniture. What is the title?
        When Mrs. Rogers tells her maid to change the
      towels, this maid uses scissors to do it! Name that
      funny book!

201. <u>Big Bad Bruce</u> by Bill Peet
        This bear is a bully who picks on the smaller animals
      ... until he meets up with Roxy the witch! Name that
      book!
        In which book does Bruce roll big rocks down the
      mountain to scare the other animals?

202. <u>The Rooster Crows</u> by Maud and Miska Petersham
        What Caldecott book has rhymes and jingles, such
      as "This Little Pig," "The Bear Went Over the Moun-
      tain" and "Fuzzy Wuzzy?"
        What Caldecott book has rhymes and jingles, finger
      games, and rope-skipping games?

203. <u>I Was a Second Grade Werewolf</u> by Daniel Manus Pink-
      water
        Lawrence Talbot runs part of the way to school on
      his hands and knees because he has turned into a were-
      wolf. Name that book!
        He eats a pencil and a milk carton; he growls; he
      bites a girl. Is he crazy? No, but he is a boy turned
      werewolf! Name that book!

204. <u>Song of the Swallows</u> by Leo Politi
        When the swallows return in spring to the Mission of
      San Juan Capistrano, young Juan and old Julian are
      there to greet them. What is the title?
        Name the picture book which shows the beautiful
      Mission of San Juan Capistrano in California, spring
      home of the swallows.

205. <u>The Tale of Peter Rabbit</u> by Beatrix Potter
        Name the book with these characters: Flopsy, Mopsy,
      Cottontail and Peter.
        This little rabbit loses his shoes and his new blue
      jacket in Mr. McGregor's garden. Name his story.

206. <u>Pop Corn and Ma Goodness</u> by Edna M. Preston
        When Ma and Pop fall down on the "slippitty sloppetty"

lane and crack heads, they fall in love and get married.
What is the title?
    In what book do Pop and Ma have a funeral for their
goat that the "b'ar" killed?

207. **The Glorious Flight Across the Channel with Lewis Bleriot** by Alice Provensen
    A broken rib, sprains, a black eye and bruises, all
from aeroplane crashes, cannot stop this man from learning how to fly. What book is he in?
    What book has eleven aeroplanes, named Bleriot I,
Bleriot II, Bleriot III, all the way through Bleriot XI,
all of which, except the last, crash?

208. **The Fool of the World and the Flying Ship** by Arthur
Ransome
    When the stupid third brother shares his lunch with
an old man, the old man tells him how to make a flying
ship. What is the name of this story?
    In what book does the Fool's friend, the Eater, eat
twelve roasted oxen and bread from forty ovens?

209. **Mrs. Pig's Bulk Buy** by Mary Rayner
    In what book does Mrs. Pig buy six enormous bottles
of tomato ketchup?
    It was ketchup for breakfast, ketchup for lunch,
ketchup for dinner and snacks. Name the book in which
ten little pigs learn to hate tomato ketchup.

210. **My Mother Is the Most Beautiful Woman in the World** by
Becky Reyher
    In what story does the village leader send for the
most beautiful women in the area to see if one is Varya's
mother?
    Varya knew who was the most beautiful woman in
the world because she saw with her heart as well as her
eyes. Name her story.

211. **Baboushka and the Three Kings** by Ruth Robbins
    When three men invite this old woman to go with them
in search of a newborn Baby, she wants to wait until
morning. Name this Christmas story.
    This book tells the story of an old woman who wants
to finish her work before she goes with three travellers
in search of a newborn Baby. Can you give the title?

212.   When I Was Young in the Mountains by Cynthia Rylant
        The girl in this book never wanted to go to the des-
ert or to the ocean because she liked where she was,
in the mountains. Can you name it?
        Name the book in which a girl remembers being
photographed with three other people and a long snake
that was draped across their necks.

213.   Journey Cake, Ho! by Ruth Sawyer
        What book has a cake that is chased by Johnny, a
cow, a duck, two sheep, a pig, some hens and a donkey?
        Name the book in which a cake brings all the animals
back to Old Merry and Grumble's home on Tip Top Mountain.

214.   Rain Makes Applesauce by Julian Scheer
        In what book do monkeys mumble in a jelly bean
jungle?
        In this book you will find tigers sleeping on an ele-
phant's snoot. Name it!

215.   Bea and Mr. Jones by Amy Schwartz
        Her father's job doesn't sound too bad to Bea, so
she takes his place in this book called....
        Bea is a big success at her father's office and her
father is the smartest student in Miss Seymour's kindergarten class. What book are they in?

216.   Outside Over There by Maurice Sendak
        While Ida plays her wonderhorn, the goblins kidnap
her little sister! What book is this?
        In what book do goblins leave a baby made of ice in
her little sister's cradle to fool Ida?

217.   Bartholomew and the Oobleck by Dr. Seuss
        King Derwin was tired of snow, fog, sunshine and
rain. He wanted something else to come down from the
sky, and it did! Name that book!
        What book tells of an ooey, gooey kind of weather
that sticks to everything--until Bartholomew comes to
the rescue?

218.   Horton Hatches the Egg by Dr. Seuss
        In what book does Mayzie the lazy bird get an ele-
phant to babysit her egg?

Even when hunters aim their guns at him, this faithful elephant stays on the egg. What book is he in?

219. How the Grinch Stole Christmas by Dr. Seuss
     This fellow hates Christmas so much, he decides to
dress up as Santa and stop the Whos' Christmas. What
is this book called?
     This Santa comes down the chimney and steals all the
stockings, presents and trees in Whoville. Can you
name the book?

220. If I Ran the Zoo by Dr. Seuss
     Gerald McGrew thinks he can make a better zoo by
finding unusual animals. Name his story.
     The zoo in this book has an Elephant-Cat and a
scraggle-foot Mulligatawny. What is the title?

221. The Lorax by Dr. Seuss
     The Once-ler is the only person who can tell you
what happened to the Truffula Trees. What book is he
in?
     In what book do the Brown Bar-ba-loots go hungry
because the Once-ler has chopped down the Truffula
Trees?

222. McElligot's Pool by Dr. Seuss
     "You'll never catch a fish here," says the farmer.
But Marco has other ideas in this picture book called....
     In which book will you find a fish made of strawberry
jelly, one with a curly nose and one that is part cow?

223. The Best Valentine in the World by Marjorie Weinman
     Sharmat
     Ferdinand Fox brings Florette Fox a big valentine
in a garbage bag. What book is this?
     Name the book in which Ferdinand Fox makes Florette
Fox a big, but purple valentine.

224. Gila Monsters Meet You at the Airport by Marjorie Wein-
     man Sharmat
     The boy in this book doesn't want to move out west
where they have chili and beans for breakfast, and
everyone is named Tex or Slim. He wants to stay in
New York City with Seymour and eat salami sandwiches.
The title is....

Name the book in which a New York City boy who
dreads moving out west meets a western boy who dreads
moving to the east.

225. The Angry Moon by William Sleator
What Indian folktale tells of Lupan's climbing to the
sky to find Lapowinsa whom the moon has kidnapped?
In which book does the moon roll after two Indian
children until it is stopped by a lake made by a fish
eye?

226. The Amazing Bone by William Steig
In what book will you find a bone that can talk in
any language and can even sneeze?
In what book does a bone say some magic words
which make a fox shrink as small as a mouse?

227. Doctor DeSoto by William Steig
What tiny dentist, who is also a mouse, refuses to
accept cats or other dangerous animals as patients?
What book has an animal dentist who is so small he
has to stand on a ladder to treat his large patients?
His name is the title of the book.

228. Sylvester and the Magic Pebble by William Steig
What book tells of a young donkey who turns into a
rock for a whole year?
Mr. and Mrs. Duncan are sure their son is dead--
until they go for a picnic on Strawberry Hill. What is
the title?

229. Daddy Is a Monster ... Sometimes by John Steptoe
Bweela and Javaka's daddy is usually nice, except
when hair grows all over his face, his teeth get long
and sharp, and he growls. Name that book!
When Bweela and Javaka behave like little monsters,
their daddy becomes a big monster. What book are
they in?

230. What's Under My Bed? by James Stevenson
Mary Ann and Louie can't get to sleep after Grandpa
tells them a scary story in this book called....
In what book does Grandpa tell Mary Ann and Louie
a story about ghosts, skeletons, bats and being scared?

231. The Planet of Lost Things by Mark Strand
        In what book does Luke travel to another planet and
      meet the Missing Person and the Unknown Soldier?
        Name the book in which Luke travels to another
      planet and finds all of the things that magicians have
      made disappear.

232. A Gift for Tia Rosa by Karen Taha
        In what book does Carmela's favorite neighbor give
      her a tiny silver rose for a present?
        Carmela wanted to give Tia Rosa a surprise, but it
      was too late. The name of this book is....

233. Many Moons by James Thurber
        Not the Lord High Chamberlain, the Royal Wizard,
      nor the Royal Mathematician can help the King get the
      moon for his sick daughter. Only the Court Jester can
      help in this book called....
        Name the fairy tale in which Princess Lenore decides
      that the moon is made of gold and can grow again just
      like a new tooth.

234. Anatole by Eve Titus
        What mouse decides to be a cheese taster so he can
      pay people back for the food he takes? His name is the
      title of the book.
        In what book does M'sieu Duval write a letter of
      thanks to a secret cheese taster?

235. Hide and Seek Fog by Alvin Tresselt
        The adults on Cape Cod don't like the fog but the
      children do. They can get lost in front of their own
      cottages! Name that book!
        Name the book in which Cape Cod's worst fog in
      twenty years makes the adults grumpy and the children
      happy.

236. Thy Friend, Obadiah by Brinton Turkle
        Name the book in which a seagull follows Obadiah
      everywhere.
        Name the book in which Obadiah untangles a rusty
      fishhook from a seagull's beak.

237. Ben's Dream by Chris Van Allsburg
        While studying his geography book, Ben falls asleep
      and goes on a strange journey. What book is he in?

In what book does Ben float past the great landmarks of the world?

238. The Garden of Abdul Gasazi by Chris Van Allsburg
      Even though the sign says, "No Dogs Allowed,"
      Fritz takes off into the garden, so Alan has to follow.
      What book is this?
      When this magician finds dogs on his property, he
      changes them into ducks. That's what happens to Fritz
      in this book called....

239. Jumanji by Chris Van Allsburg
      Name the book about a board game found in the
      park that is much too real!
      Judy and Peter are not bored any longer when they
      find a very unusual jungle adventure game. Name that
      book!

240. Ira Sleeps Over by Bernard Waber
      When Ira spends the night at his friend's house for
      the first time, he has a big problem. Can you name
      his story?
      Spending the night with Reggie is fun--until the
      boys begin telling ghost stories. Name that book!

241. Lyle, Lyle Crocodile by Bernard Waber
      When Lyle smiles his toothy smile at Loretta, it
      scares her, and she dislikes him even more than before.
      What book are they in?
      No matter what Lyle does, he just can't please Mr.
      Grumps and his cat, Loretta, in this book called....

242. A Chair for My Mother by Vera B. Williams
      When the big jar is full of money, this little girl and
      her mother will buy a chair to replace the one that was
      burned with their house. What book are they in?
      Because a fire burned all their furniture, mama
      doesn't have a good place to take a load off her feet,
      so the family is saving change to buy her a chair.
      Name that book.

243. Three Days on a River in a Red Canoe by Vera B. Wil-
      liams
      Aunt Rosie, Mom and two kids drive all day to reach
      a special place where they will begin their canoe trip.
      Can you name their story?

What book tells about a canoe trip and has a recipe
for fruit stew and dumplings?

244. Crow Boy by Taro Yashima
Chibi is ignored at school for six years until kind
Mr. Isobe becomes the teacher. What is the title?
After being teased and ignored for six years, shy
Chibi finally earns the children's admiration for his
unusual talent. Name that book!

245. Seashore Story by Taro Yashima
Can you name the story of Urashima the fisherman
and how he rides on a turtle to the bottom of the sea?
Urashima stays so long under the sea with the turtle,
that when he returns to his village, he can't find anyone he knows. What is the title?

246. The Emperor and the Kite by Jane Yolen
In what book does a small princess keep her father
alive in a tower by flying food to him on her kite?
What book tells of a tiny princess who rescues her
father from a tower by flying a rope to him on her kite?

247. Duffy and the Devil: A Cornish Tale by Harve Zemach
When the maid can't figure out how to spin the yarn
for Squire Lovel's stockings, a strange creature with
horns and a long tail offers to make a deal with her.
What is the title of the book?
Squire Lovel is very proud of Duffy's spinning and
knitting but he doesn't know that she isn't the one
doing it. What book is this?

248. The Judge by Harve Zemach
Five prisoners are sent to jail in this book for telling
a tale about a scary thing coming toward the town.
What is the title?
Name the book in which a judge gets eaten up by a
monster with horns, wings and a long tail.

249. The Meanest Squirrel I Ever Met by Gene Zion
In what book does Mr. M.O. Squirrel teach Nibbles
how to play "Nut in the Hat"?
Nibbles and his family have to eat Thanksgiving dinner at a restaurant because someone stole their dinner
nuts! Name that book!

250. <u>William's Doll</u> by Charlotte Zolotow
        The boy next door thinks William is a sissy for want-
ing a doll. What book are they in?
        In this book a boy's father buys him a basketball
and an electric train so he will forget about wanting a
doll. Name his story.

CHAPTER III

FOURTH GRADE

EASIER READING

251. Freckle Juice by Judy Blume
     Andrew Marcus wants freckles more than anything.
     He even wants them badly enough to spend five weeks
     allowance to get them! Name his story.
     In which book does Andrew Marcus come to school
     with blue dots all over his face?

252. Dumb Old Casey Is a Fat Tree by Barbara Bottner
     Casey has always wanted to be a ballet dancer, but
     they don't take fat girls! What book is Casey in?
     Casey is hoping to get the part of the evil prince
     in the ballet recital, but she ends up as only a tree.
     Name that book!

253. Floramel and Esteban by Emilie Buchwald
     Name the book in which Rafie refuses to sell his cow,
     even though he is offered 2000 silver coins for her!
     In what book is a cow named Floramel so special that
     a song is written about her?

254. A Certain Small Shepherd by Rebecca Caudill
     The night Jamie was born, his mother died. Now
     Jamie is just like any other boy, except for one thing--
     he can't talk. What book is he in?
     Miss Creech, the teacher, made Jamie a caroler for
     the Christmas play. But how can he sing if he can't
     even talk? Name that book!

255. Did You Carry the Flag Today, Charley? by Rebecca
     Caudill
     When Charley wears his Uncle Hawk's special hat to

the Little School, he finds he can't have any fun because someone might snatch it if he doesn't hold it on
his head. Name his story.

Charley doesn't think library books should stand on
the shelves with their backs to you, so he carefully
turns all of the books on the bottom shelf around.
What is the title of this book?

256. Ellen Tebbits by Beverly Cleary
After boasting about being a good horseback rider,
Ellen finds herself in the middle of a stream on a horse
who thinks he's boss! What is the name of this funny
book?

Because of Ellen's terrible secret, she hides in the
broom closet to dress for ballet lessons. Name her
story.

257. Henry Huggins by Beverly Cleary
Henry is overjoyed that his mother said he could
keep the skinny dog he found in the drugstore, but his
troubles start when he has to bring him home on the
bus. Name that book!

In what book does a boy start out with a pair of
guppies and soon have hundreds, or even thousands,
of guppies and nowhere to put them?

258. Mitch and Amy by Beverly Cleary
These fourth-grade twins are not alike at all. The
sister is great in reading and hates multiplication, and
her brother is in the lowest reading group but he's
great in math. What is the title of their story?

Even though the Huff twins quarrel a lot, Mitchell
knows he can't let a big bully get away with spitting
in his sister's hair. Name that book!

259. Ramona Forever by Beverly Cleary
Name the book in which Ramona Quimby is going to
become a middle child instead of the baby of the family.

At their aunt's wedding, the Quimby girls get rid
of their too tight shoes by tying them to the back of
a truck. Name that book!

260. Ramona Quimby, Age 8 by Beverly Cleary
There are two ways to open hardboiled eggs at this
girl's school. You are either a rapper or a whacker.

In what book does this eight-year-old girl live to regret being a whacker?

In what book does a teacher tell the children in class to hold their noses and file into the hall because Ramona threw up?

261. Ramona the Brave by Beverly Cleary
     In this book, Ramona gets a new bedroom of her own, but after six months, she must trade bedrooms with Beezus. Can you name the book?

     In what book will you find first-grader Ramona so mad at Susan for copying her owl that she throws her own away and crumples Susan's owl just before Parents' Night?

262. My Mother Is the Smartest Woman in the World by Eleanor Clymer
     Sometimes she wears blue jeans and sneakers, sometimes a green dress and earrings, but she's always Richard's and Kathleen's mom and she's running for mayor in this book called....

     Name the book in which Kathleen doesn't know how much her life will change because she has talked her mother into running for mayor.

263. Ivan the Great by Isabel Langis Cusack
     No one in his family believes Robbie is telling the truth except his parrot. The parrot's name is the title of this book. Do you know it?

     Can you name the book in which a boy named Robbie gets a very unusual parrot for a pet?

264. The Magic Finger by Roald Dahl
     In what book does the entire Gregg family shrink in size and grow wings instead of arms?

     In this book the Gregg family finds out what it's like to have duck wings, live in a nest, and be shot at. Can you name it?

265. The Bears on Hemlock Mountain by Alice Dalgliesh
     Bear tracks in the snow around the big iron pot where Jonathon was hiding prove that his mother was wrong and Jonathon was right. What is the title?

     When Jonathon sees bears coming, he crawls into the only safe place he knows--a big iron cooking pot. What is the title of the story?

266. A Toad for Tuesday by Russell Erickson
     In what book does Warton set off to take some beetle
     brittle to his Aunt Toolia and run into danger from a
     mean, nasty owl?
     Name the book in which Warton is to be eaten for an
     owl's birthday treat the following Tuesday.

267. Warton and the Traders by Russell Erickson
     In what book does a toad save two wood rats from
     a wildcat?
     When Warton finally finds his lost Aunt Toolia, she
     is in a very dangerous place for a toad--the bog--and
     she won't leave. What book is she in?

268. Finzel the Farsighted by Paul Fleischman
     Finzel can tell fortunes and see people's futures but
     his eyesight is so bad that he spends an entire summer
     trying to shoo the plums off his plum tree because he
     thinks they are birds. Name that book!
     Name the book in which Finzel catches a thief by
     cutting open an onion.

269. McBroom and the Beanstalk by Sid Fleischman
     In which book does Josh McBroom enter the World
     Champion Liar's Contest at the county fair?
     When the McBroom children throw a bean out the
     window, it grows into an enormous stalk that takes
     over the town. Name the book!

270. McBroom Tells a Lie by Sid Fleischman
     In which book do Josh McBroom's children plant a
     crop of Mexican jumping beans on the farm?
     In this funny book the hens eat Mexican jumping
     beans and lay eggs that flip themselves in the frying
     pan. Can you name the book?

271. The Beast in Mrs. Rooney's Room by Patricia Reilly Giff
     What book has a boy named Richard Best who calls
     himself Beast?
     Richard Best is retained in second grade and goes to
     a special reading teacher in this book called....

272. Mustard by Charlotte Graeber
     Alex's cat is fourteen years old and Dr. Griffith says
     he must take things easy and have no excitement or
     stress. What book is he in?

Name the book in which Jeff Reed's dog causes Alex's cat to have a heart attack.

273. <u>Eating Ice Cream with A Werewolf</u> by Phyllis Green
     Brad Gowan's babysitter, Phoebe Hadley, claims to be a witch. She wears a lavender jump suit with a matching cape that touches the floor and carries a stuffed black cat because she is allergic to real cats. Can you name this book?
     Chickens, a quiet picnic spot, werewolves, boyfriends and ice cream--these things are part of magic spells conjured up by Brad Gowan and his babysitter Phoebe. Name that book!

274. <u>Give Us a Great Big Smile, Rosie Cole</u> by Sheila Greenwald
     Rosie is ten now and it's time for Uncle Ralph to write a book about her special talent, just as he did for her sisters. The problem is, Rosie has no talent. Can you name that book?
     Can you name the book in which a girl plays the violin so badly that the neighbors accuse her family of having a wild cat or an electric saw in their apartment?

275. <u>Betsy's Play School</u> by Carolyn Haywood
     Name the book in which Betsy pours a pitcher of lemonade over Fay's head to put out a fire.
     Rodney can have the tiny black poodle for his very own if he can remember where he put the winning ticket, number nine. Name that book!

276. <u>The Problem with Pulcifer</u> by Florence Parry Heide
     In this book, Pulcifer is considered a troublemaker because he would rather read than watch TV. What is its title?
     Name the book in which Pulcifer is sent to a special remedial class for students who don't like to watch TV.

277. <u>Saint George and the Dragon</u> by Margaret Hodges
     This brave knight saves Una's kingdom from a terrible fire-breathing dragon. Can you name his story?
     Una thinks the dragon has killed the Red Cross Knight, but as the knight rests in the silvery water, his wounds heal. What book is this?

278. Much Ado About Aldo by Johanna Hurwitz
        To save the crickets from being eaten, Aldo hides
four chameleons in the teacher's desk. Name that book!
        Name the book in which a third-grader decides to
become a vegetarian because of a science experiment
with crickets and chameleons.

279. Rip-Roaring Russell by Johanna Hurwitz
        Name the book in which Russell's best friend, Jeremy,
causes him to lose his two front teeth.
        Russell's mother is upset because he calls a boy in
his nursery school class "Germy." Later she discovers
that Russell isn't being rude, he just can't pronounce
Jeremy in this book called....

280. The Mona Lisa Mystery by Pat Hutchins
        Mr. Jones and his third-grade class are very excited
about their upcoming trip to Paris, but a gang of thieves
is even more excited because they plan to use the children to steal a famous painting from the Louvre. Name
that book!
        Avril and her third-grade classmates chase a man
with a gun who has just stolen a famous painting. A
shot is heard, and Avril falls to the ground moaning.
Name that book!

281. No One Is Going to Nashville by Mavis Jukes
        Sonia's dad won't let her keep the stray dog because
all of her other pets have wounded him. The title of
this book is....
        Ms. Mackey, the goose, and Fangs, the Alligator
Lizard, are two of Sonia's many pets. Now she wants
to keep a stray dog. What book is this?

282. Seven Kisses in a Row by Patricia MacLachlan
        Divided grapefruit with a cherry in the middle is
the favorite breakfast of Emma, a little girl in this
book entitled....
        Uncle Elliot and Aunt Evelyn are about to become
parents, so they practice parenting by taking care of
Emma and her brother, Zachary, while their parents
are away. Name that book.

283. Caroline and Her Kettle Named Maud by Miriam Mason
        Name the book in which a frontier girl named Caroline

wants a gun for her birthday even though guns aren't
for girls.
   Caroline tries to find seven four-leaf clovers that
grow near gray rocks because she thinks they would
be magic and grant her birthday wish in this book
called....

284. Annie and the Old One by Miska Miles
   So that her mother will have to come to school instead of weave the rug, Annie throws the teacher's shoe
in the trash can. Name that book!
   In this book, an Indian girl tries to stop her grandmother from dying by pulling out the weaving of a rug
each night. What book is this?

285. Long Meg by Rosemary Minard
   In what book does a girl named Meg dress like a
man so that she can be a soldier and fight in France?
   What book has a woman in it who is as tall as the
tallest man in the town of Westminster and a better
sword fighter than any man?

286. The Strange Thing That Happened to Oliver Wendell
Iscovitch by Helen Kronberg Olson
   Oliver Wendell Iscovitch has the roundest, pinkest
cheeks anyone has ever seen. Name the book in which
his cheeks cause him to float when he holds his breath.
   When this boy holds his breath because his mother
won't buy him Goody Woody Cereal, his cheeks get very
fat and round and an amazing thing happens in this book
called....

287. Rolling Harvey down the Hill by Jack Prelutsky
   Name the book in which Harvey ties two of his friends
to trees, pulls down their pants, then leaves.
   In what book do four friends gang up on a mean boy
named Harvey?

288. Mr. Yowder and the Train Robbers by Glen Rounds
   If you were stuck in the bottom of a well, you would
be glad to have friends who were long and skinny and
could tie knots in themselves so you could use them to
climb out. In what book does a sign painter escape
danger in just this way?

In this book, Mr. Yowder and his snake buddies team
up to fool a gang of robbers. What's the title?

289. Mr. Yowder and the Windwagon by Glen Rounds
        Can you name the book in which a man and his pos-
      sible investor passengers drive a windwagon through
      a herd of buffalo before becoming stranded in the middle
      of the Great Plains?
        Even though his first windbuggy experiment ends in
      disaster, Mr. Yowder is still determined to make a wind-
      powered covered wagon in this book called....

290. Ike and Mama and the Once-a-Year Suit by Carol Snyder
        Everyone in the Bronx wears a bag filled with garlic
      around their neck to keep them from getting the flu.
      But Ike forgets to wear his on a shopping trip with his
      mother. What book is he in?
        Ike really wants the dark blue suit he sees in the
      store but he makes one mistake while shopping with his
      mother and now he's afraid that she won't buy him the
      suit. Can you name that book?

291. Molly McCullough and Tom the Rogue by Kathleen Stevens
        In exchange for supper, Tom tells farmers stories of
      his travels. Then he buys land from the farmer knowing
      that the next day he will sell the land back to the farmer
      for more than he paid. What is the title of this book?
        Farmer McCollough's daughter is very ugly and has a
      sharp tongue but she proves herself to be smarter than
      any man in this book called....

292. Ty's One-Man Band by Mildred Pitts Walter
        Wooden spoons, a comb, a tin pail and a washboard--
      all are used to make music in this book called....
        In what book does Ty meet a peg-legged man who
      claims to be able to make music with a comb?

293. The Jazz Man by Mary H. Weik
        Zeke hid in the closet when the school man came,
      then sat in his room watching the window across the
      way with the newly painted yellow walls. One wonder-
      ful day someone special moved in there and changed
      Zeke's life. Name that book!
        After his parents leave him, nine-year-old Zeke's
      thoughts turn to the man with the piano and his friends,

Tony, Manuel and Ernie, who make music in the apartment with the yellow walls. What is the title?

294. The Crystal Child by Barbara Wersba
Name the book in which something so terrible happens to a little girl that she turns into a crystal statue. Because the boy visits the beautiful statue every day, the old gardener finally tells the boy about the legend of the crystal statue in this book called....

ADVANCED READING

295. Footsteps on the Stairs by Carole S. Adler
In an effort to impress her new stepsister and brother, Dodie, in a white sheet and with white cream on her face, leans out the window moaning as they drive up with her parents. She scares her seven-year-old stepbrother so badly that he won't get out of the car. Name that book!
When Dodie sees the rented house where she will spend her summer vacation, she thinks it looks creepy, like a haunted house for vampires. She's right! The ghosts of two sisters who drowned stalk the house late at night. Can you name that book?

296. A Month of Sundays by Rose Blue
Mr. Hart, the teacher of Class 5-205, was different from any teacher Jeffrey had ever known. He wore turtlenecks and a peace medal and rode a motorcycle. What book is he in?
Ten-year-old Jeffrey moves to New York City with his mother when his parents get a divorce. In what book does Jeffrey ask if his friend Matthew's mother could be his mother too?

297. Superfudge by Judy Blume
Because his kindergarten teacher refuses to call Farley Drexler by his nickname, he calls her Rat Face and is sent to the principal. Can you name the book?
Will his baby sister's toes come off? In which book does Farley Drexler Hatcher know just how to find out?

298. Tales of a Fourth Grade Nothing by Judy Blume
When Peter Hatcher wins a pet turtle at a birthday

party, he is delighted until Dribble gets eaten by Peter's
little brother. What is the title of this book?
    Peter's little brother gets all the breaks. In which
book does he get a job making a toddle-bike commercial
for TV?

299. Devil's Donkey by Bill Brittain
    In this book Dan'l Pitt never thought he'd end up
in a tug-o-war with the devil, but he did! Can you
name it?
    In what book does Old Magda, the witch, turn Daniel
into a donkey?

300. The Ghost of Windy Hill by Clyde Robert Bulla
    Lorna and Jamie decide that their house is not really
haunted, but the countryside holds very strange characters, such as Miss Miggie and Tench, the beggar
boy's father. What book tells their story?
    First Lorna hears knocking in the night, then her
half-finished quilt disappears. Name that book!

301. Shoeshine Girl by Clyde Robert Bulla
    Sarah Ida thinks her aunt won't let her work in the
shoeshine stand, but Aunt Claudia doesn't even care!
What is the title of this book?
    Sarah Ida shouted at Al as he crossed the street,
but it was too late. In what book does Al give her
the key to his business as he waits for the ambulance?

302. The Eighteenth Emergency by Betsy Byars
    Marv Hammerman, the school bully, is after our friend
Mouse, and Mouse decides to face him and get it over
with. What book is this?
    Garbage Dog will eat anything. In which book do
Benjie and Ezzie discover a live turtle in his mouth?

303. The Night the Monster Came by Mary Calhoun
    Andy is alone in the house at night. He switches
on the outside light and there in the snow by the
garbage can are giant footprints. Can you name the
book in which Andy thinks Bigfoot left the footprints?
    Andy's house is the last house on Meadowlark Lane.
Beyond his house are the Great North Woods where Bigfoot and the Windigo are rumored to live. Can you name
this book in which Andy is afraid to stay alone in the
house?

304. The Chocolate Touch by Patrick Catling
        John Midas never thought he could get enough
      chocolate, but he changes his mind in this book called....
        John Midas finds a strange coin with a picture of a
      fat boy on one side and the initials, J.M., on the other.
      In what book does he use the coin to buy candy from
      an unusual candy shop?

305. Earthstar Magic by Ruth Chew
        Trudy the witch is so bad at magic, she is expelled
      from the witch coven and has to give up her hat and
      broom. Name her story.
        In which book does Ben shrink so small that a mother
      bird feeds him to her baby?

306. Dear Mr. Henshaw by Beverly Cleary
        Someone in his classroom is stealing the good things
      from Leigh Bott's lunchbox. Can you name the book in
      which Leigh invents a burglar alarm and places it in his
      lunch box to catch the thief?
        Leigh Botts writes to his favorite author and encloses
      a list of ten questions for him to answer. In what book
      does the author answer Leigh's letter and include ten
      questions for Leigh to answer?

307. The Mouse and the Motorcycle by Beverly Cleary
        Name the book in which a mouse lies trapped at the
      bottom of a wastebasket with only an apple core and a
      toy motorcycle to keep him company.
        In what book does a mouse get his own special room
      service to deliver a peanut butter and jelly sandwich?

308. Otis Spofford by Beverly Cleary
        Which book is named after its main character, a boy
      who wears glow-in-the-dark shoelaces--pink on the right
      and green on the left?
        This boy's teacher makes him throw spitballs into the
      wastebasket until he runs out of spit. If you can name
      him, you will know the title.

309. Ralph S. Mouse by Beverly Cleary
        The newspaper headline read, "Class Nabs Sneed In-
      vader." Who or what is the strange invader of Irwin J.
      Sneed Elementary School? The invader's name is the
      name of this book. Do you know it?

Some people call this mouse a mouse in a million,
because he can ride a motorcycle and can talk. But
not everyone can understand him, only lonely children
who listen carefully. Other children think he just
squeaks funny. Can you name this book?

310. Ramona and Her Father by Beverly Cleary
      In this book, Mr. Quimby loses his job, Mrs. Quimby
gets full-time work, and Ramona and Beezus begin a
campaign to make their father quit smoking. Name that
book!
      When Picky-Picky the cat attacks their Jack-o-lantern,
the Quimby's end up eating pumpkin pie and pumpkin
custard until they never want to see another pumpkin
again. What book is this?

311. Ramona and Her Mother by Beverly Cleary
      In which book does seven-and-a-half-year-old Ramona
give Willa Jean Kemp a box of pink Kleenex for a present?
      Angry and disappointed at her sewing, Ramona makes
herself feel better by squeezing out a whole tube of
toothpaste into the wash basin. Name that book!

312. Runaway Ralph by Beverly Cleary
      In this book Ralph the mouse goes to Happy Acres
Camp and finds himself the object of a tomcat's lesson
on how to handle a mouse. What is the title?
      This mouse watches television all day and rides a
motorcycle all night in the Mountain View Inn. Name
the book in which he decides to leave and ends up in a
summer camp for kids.

313. Socks by Beverly Cleary
      What little kitten with four white paws finds himself
on a pile of letters at the bottom of a mailbox? His
name is the title of the book.
      This tabby cat feels nobody loves him anymore since
the new baby's arrival in the Bricker family. And now
the Brickers are even putting him on a diet! What is
the title?

314. Help! I'm a Prisoner in the Library by Eth Clifford
      The two sisters, Mary Rose and Jo-Beth Onetree,
realize they are locked in a rather spooky library when

the lights go out. A little later they hear a loud thump
and something starts making moaning noises. Can you
name this book?

Mary Rose Onetree is only ten, so the police and
fire departments think she is playing a prank when she
tells them that she and her sister are locked in a library.
What book is this?

315. Me and the Eggman by Eleanor Clymer
When Donald discovers he is locked in the egg and
vegetable man's panel truck, he realizes that running
away from home is the dumbest thing he has ever done.
Name that book!
Donald Walker thinks his family's apartment is awful.
It is so small that someone has to sleep in every room.
in what book does he run away from home when bossy
Aunt Lizzie moves in with them?

316. Mishmash by Molly Cone
This dog likes to eat cake at the table with Mrs.
Peters and her guests and help the mailman deliver
letters. What book is he in?
When Pete Peters tries to take the big black dog
back to his former owner, he finds the man has moved
--house and all! What is the name of this book?

317. Me and the Terrible Two by Ellen Conford
Dorrie doesn't think life is fair. The awful Haskell
twins have just moved in next door where Marlene, her
best friend, used to live. Name that book!
In what book does Dorrie Kimball receive a $7.00
medical bill from Conrad Haskell? The bill is for tran-
quilizers for his guinea pig.

318. The Baseball Trick by Scott Corbett
When Fenton Claypool, the Panthers' star pitcher,
dreams of being a home-run hitter, too, Kerby looks
to Mrs. Graymalkin for help. Name that book!
In what book do Kerby, Bumps, and Fenton discover
that Red Blake has imported some big boys from across
town so the Wildcats can beat the Panthers at baseball?

319. The Disappearing Dog Trick by Scott Corbett
In this book Mrs. Graymalkin tells Kerby how to
mix up a chemical solution that will help him find Waldo,
his dog. Can you name the book?

In what book does Waldo, without his collar and tags, get picked up by the dogcatcher?

320. The Lemonade Trick by Scott Corbett
      To his parents' amazement, Kerby spends all day being good and helpful. Only he knows it is because of his new magic chemistry set. Name that book!
      In what book does Kerby use his dog Waldo to test a chemical mixture that makes you want to be good?

321. The Courage of Sarah Noble by Alice Dalgliesh
      In what book does an eight-year-old go with her father into the wilds of Connecticut to cook for him while he builds a house? The title of this book comes from something her mother told her when she left home.
      In this book, set in the pioneer days, eight-year-old Sarah finds out that Indian mothers can be just as loving as her own. What is the title?

322. Valley of the Ponies by Jean Slaughter Doty
      Jennifer is sure her summer is ruined because her parents are taking her to New England for vacation, away from her job and lessons at the local riding stable. In what book does the owner of the stable call with a solution to her problems?
      Modern day horse thieves steal horses for packing plants to butcher. When Jennifer stumbles onto thieves loading her neighbor's horses onto a truck, she doesn't know how to stop them. Name that book!

323. The Hundred Dresses by Eleanor Estes
      Wanda sometimes tells the other girls about the many clothes in her closet at home, yet she wears the same dress to school day after day. Name that book!
      In what book does a little girl have many, many dresses--none of which she can wear?

324. The Skates of Uncle Richard by Carol Fenner
      Instead of the beautiful white ice skates she wants for Christmas, Marsha gets hand-me-down, ugly black skates. What book is she in?
      Marsha's dream is to be an ice skater, but she keeps falling down, until uncle Richard shows her how to lace her skates correctly. Name that book!

325. Phoebe Danger, Detective, in the Case of the Two-
     Minute Cough by Paul Fleischmann
          Name the book in which Phoebe and her friend Dash
     decide to form their own detective agency.
          Phoebe and Dash are detectives. Name the book in
     which their first case involves a bottle of priceless cough
     syrup.

326. The Ghost on Saturday Night by Sid Fleischman
          When Opie guides a big ugly stranger to the hotel,
     his payment is a ticket for two to a ghost-raising. What
     book is he in?
          In what book does the ghost of Crookneck John es-
     cape his coffin and send everyone running, everyone
     but Aunt Etta and Opie?

327. Stone Fox by John Reynolds Gardiner
          In what book will you meet little Willie, a dog named
     Searchlight and a grandfather who loses his will to live?
          Little Willie and Searchlight have to win the dog-sled
     race, but they're racing against the best dogs in the
     country, in this book called....

328. Fourth Grade Celebrity by Patricia Reilly Giff
          By mistake, Casey Valentine's made-up story of how
     she saves her school from a fire is published in the
     school newspaper. Name that book!
          Name the book in which Casey Valentine takes her
     sister's wooden-bead necklace to give to Darlene for
     her birthday and then discovers that the necklace was
     a Christmas present to her sister from Darlene's sister.

329. Left-Handed Shortstop by Patricia Reilly Giff
          Name the book in which Walter Moles puts a fake
     papier mâché cast on his left arm so he won't have to
     play baseball.
          What book has a character called Rat Teeth who is
     the best baseball player in fifth grade?

330. 4B Goes Wild by Jamie Gilson
          Even though this fourth grade class put a fish be-
     tween the principal's sheets, they still get a reward
     for good behavior--three days at Outdoor Ed Camp.
     What book are they in?

In what book do the members of a certain fourth-
grade class "truck" each other with flashlights during
Outdoor Ed camp?

331. Thirteen Ways to Sink a Sub by Jamie Gilson
      In order to win their bet with the girls, the boys
of room 4B must be first to make their substitute teacher
cry. If they lose the bet they have to retrieve balls
from the playground's dreaded spit pit for the rest of
of the year. Name that book!
      A search for a nonexistent contact lens, a boy who
pretends to be Japanese and a paper towel stuffed in
a sink's drain are all part of 4B's strategy to make
their substitute teacher cry in this book called....

332. Incognito Mosquito, Private Insective by E.A. Hass
      What book has the following characters: Inspector
Insector, Glorious Vanderbug and Vidal Cocoon? Clue:
All the characters are insects.
      Can you name the book in which a famous detective
is a mosquito?

333. Bunnicula; A Rabbit Tale of Mystery by Deborah and
James Howe
      Harold the dog tells the spooky story of a little rab-
bit found in a movie theater and the strange goings-on
in the Monroe household after he arrives. Name that
book!
      The baby rabbit has strange markings on his back
like a cape, and his teeth don't look quite right. Name
the book in which Chester the cat decides to get to the
bottom of this mystery.

334. Howliday Inn by James Howe
      Abandoned! That's how Harold feels when Chester
and he are boarded at Chateau Bow-Wow while the Monroe family is on vacation. This book is called....
      Harold and Chester know that something isn't quite
right at Chateau Bow-Wow. In fact, Chester thinks
there may be werewolves there! Name that book!

335. Aldo Ice Cream by Johanna Hurwitz
      More than anything else, nine-year-old Aldo wants
to get $49.96 to buy his sister Karen a birthday present,
a machine that makes ice cream. In what book does he
decide to devote his entire summer to earning the money?

Aldo wants to win the Grubby-Sneaker Contest so much that he buries his sneakers in the garden every night so they will keep getting grubby, even while he sleeps. Can you name that book?

336. Baseball Fever by Johanna Hurwitz
Ezra's father loves chess and wins everytime until Ezra learns to sit on his hands in this book called....
In what book does Ezra's father agree to attend a baseball game if Ezra can beat him in a game of chess?

337. Striped Ice Cream by Joan Lexau
Being the youngest of five children means Becky gets only the handed-down clothes, but Mama is determined not to go on Welfare. What is the title?
Becky goes out because her older sisters don't want her around, and lands her very first job, babysitting Freddie for twenty-five cents an hour. Name her story.

338. Mrs. Piggle Wiggle by Betty MacDonald
This very small woman lives in a house that is upside-down; the ceiling is the floor and the chandelier is used for a campfire. Her name is the name of this book. Do you know it?
This woman loves all children and she has magic cures for their bad behavior. Her name is the name of this book. What is it?

339. Be a Perfect Person in Just Three Days! by Stephen Manes
Milo Crinkley wants to be perfect. According to Dr. K. Pinkerton Silverfish, Milo will become perfect if he does three things: wear broccoli around his neck, not eat for one day, and do nothing for 24 hours except sip weak tea. Can you name that book?
At school Milo tells everyone he has to wear broccoli on a string around his neck because of doctor's orders. If you've read this book you know the real reason he wears the broccoli. Can you name the title?

340. My Dad Lives in a Downtown Hotel by Peggy Mann
Joey Grant thought that if he was very, very good, his dad might come back to live with them. Name his story.
When his dad walks out, Joey Grant is sure it is all

his fault, so he sets out to get him back.   Name that
book!

341.   The Hundred Penny Box by Sharon Bell Mathis
       Aunt Dew was born in 1874.   In what book does
she keep a penny for each year of her life?
       No matter what, Michael won't let his mother burn
Aunt Dew's box in the furnace.   Name his story.

342.   The Secret Life of the Underwear Champ by Betty Miles
       Larry is upset because he has to make an underwear
commercial for TV and all his friends will see it.   What
book is he in?
       Larry thinks it might be okay to do a commercial for
television.   Then he finds out that he will only be wearing his underwear.   Name that book!

343.   Operation: Dump the Chump by Barbara Park
       In what book does little Robert write "Poopoo Hed"
on every single one of Oscar's Christmas cards?
       The first time Oscar holds Robert, his new baby
brother, Robert goes to the bathroom on Oscar's lap.
From then on, Oscar knows Robert will always be a
creep.   Name that book.

344.   Skinnybones by Barbara Park
       When you're such a bad player that the only way to
go is up, the Little League gives you its Most Improved
Player trophy.   In what book has Alex Frankovitch won
that trophy for the last six years?
       Name the book in which Alex Frankovitch is counted
out during a baseball game because he screams "Booga
Booga" at the pitcher.

345.   Banjo by Robert Newton Peck
       Last night Alvin Dickinson told his little sister a
bed-time story about Jake Horse who creeps around at
night looking through windows for little girls to eat.
The story even scared him and now one of his classmates wants Alvin to find Jake and use him for a school
assignment!   Name that book!
       Ferguson Byler is the least popular kid in school,
perhaps because he's filthy, smells awful and has forty-
three holes in his shirt.   One day, in a fit of pity, Alvin Dickinson picks him to be his partner for a school
assignment in this book called....

346. Fat Men from Space by Daniel Manus Pinkwater
     This book is about William, a boy with a one-in-a-
     million radio tooth. Can you name it?
     Can you name the book in which William is captured
     by a spaceburger from the planet Spiegal?

347. Veronica the Show-Off by Nancy Robinson
     Name the book in which Veronica throws a screaming
     fit because the librarian let someone else check out the
     latest Polly Winkler mystery.
     In what book does Melody Hicks send Veronica a
     secret message hidden in a library book?

348. The Bear's House by Marilyn Sachs
     Her classmates don't like Fran Ellen because she
     sucks her thumb and smells bad, but they don't know
     that there is no adult at home able to take care of her
     and her sisters and brother. Name the book.
     Ten-year-old Fran Ellen's real house is dirty and
     sad with no father and a sick mother. So Fran Ellen
     feels better in her make-believe house at the back of
     the classroom. What is the title of this book?

349. Chester by Mary Francis Shura
     Until a red-haired, freckle-faced, bicycle-riding,
     fast-running boy moves into the neighborhood, Jamie and
     her friends have their own sort of GUINNESS BOOK OF
     WORLD RECORDS. What is the title of this book?
     Jamie no longer has the most freckles, nor Amy the
     most brothers and sisters; Edie no longer has the bald-
     est baby, nor Zack the most pets. Also George is no
     longer the fastest runner--all because of the new boy
     whose name is the title of this book. What is it?

350. The Real Thief by William Steig
     Since only Gawain the goose and the King himself
     have keys to the treasury, Gawain is accused when the
     treasure disappears. Which book is this?
     Derek the mouse knows who really took the King's
     jewels, but he doesn't have the courage to speak up at
     Gawain's trial, so all he can do is keep stealing to prove
     Gawain innocent. Name his story.

351. Trouble for Lucy by Carla Stevens
     What book tells of the Stewart family, and especially

of Lucy, as they make their way to Oregon Territory in
a covered wagon during the early 1800's?
Lucy Stewart leaves the wagon train to find her lost
puppy, Finn, gets caught in a hail storm and picked up
by Pawnee Indians. Name her story.

352. Song of the Trees by Mildred Taylor
If Cassie's mother doesn't let Mr. Andersen cut down
their trees, her daddy may have a very bad accident.
Name that book!
Cassie's papa is willing to blow up their forest before he will let Mr. Andersen cut it down for lumber,
in this book called....

353. By the Shores of Silver Lake by Laura Ingalls Wilder
When Laura is almost thirteen, she and her family
take the train for the first time in their lives to join
Pa in the Dakota Territory. Name the book.
As the Ingalls family moves farther west to Dakota
Territory, Laura "sees out loud" for Mary, who is blind
from scarlet fever. Name that book!

354. Little House in the Big Woods by Laura Ingalls Wilder
When butchering time came at Laura's log cabin in
the Wisconsin woods, she plugged her ears so she
couldn't hear the hog squeal. Which book is this?
In what book do five-year-old Laura and her family
go to Grandpa's for maple syrup and a sugaring-off
dance?

355. Little House on the Prairie by Laura Ingalls Wilder
In what book does Mr. Edwards have to bring Christ-
mas presents on his head across the rising creek to
Mary, Laura, and baby Carrie?
In what book do Laura and her entire family come
down with fever 'n ague on the Kansas prairie?

356. Little Town on the Prairie by Laura Ingalls Wilder
In this book Laura's parents take Mary to a college
for blind students, and Laura is in charge of the house
for a week. Can you name it?
In which book does Nellie Oleson get fourteen-year-
old Laura into such trouble with Almanzo's sister, Miss
Wilder, that Laura and Carrie are sent home from school?

357. On the Banks of Plum Creek by Laura Ingalls Wilder
        In which book does Laura's father trade his ponies,
      a mule colt and a wagon cover for good wheat-growing
      land and a dugout house beside a creek?
        What book tells of Pete the ox almost falling through
      the roof of the Ingalls' home in Minnesota?

358. Mitzi and the Terrible Tyrannosaurus Rex by Barbara
      Williams
        In what book does Charles Darwin Potts wear blue
      swim fins because they are his dinosaur feet?
        Name the book in which Mitzi wants her mother to
      marry Mr. Ledgard, her school's janitor, instead of Wal-
      ter, because Mr. Ledgard has a motorcycle?

359. The Velveteen Rabbit; or, How Toys Become Real by
      Margery Williams
        The nursery magic Fairy turns old playthings into
      Real, in this book called....
        In what book does the Skin Horse tell his little friend
      about nursery magic and how it made him Real?

CHAPTER IV

FIFTH GRADE

EASIER READING

360. The Stone Walkers by Vivien Alcock
    Poppy Brown finds a chain made of greenish-black metal. When she puts it around the ankle of a statue named Belladonna, the statue comes to life. Name that book!
    It's common knowledge that Poppy Brown is a liar. She loves to tell lies and does so often. That's why no one believes her story about a statue that comes to life. But this time Poppy is telling the truth. Name that book!

361. Mr. Popper's Penguins by Richard and Florence Atwater
    Name the book in which a housepainter keeps penguins in his ice box.
    In what book does a man who loves penguins mail order three and put them in his bathtub and sometimes on ice in his refrigerator?

362. Knee-Knock Rise by Natalie Babbitt
    In what book does a boy named Egan set out to find a practical explanation for the unearthly moans that come from the nearby mountains?
    The village of Instep is terrified of the Megrimum, a mysterious something that lurks on a nearby mountain. Can you name that book?

363. Where the Buffaloes Begin by Olaf Baker
    Name the book in which Little Wolf wakes up to see the lake full of buffaloes.
    According to this Indian legend, Little Wolf, a ten-year-old boy, saved his people by leading a great herd of buffaloes over their enemies. Can you name it?

364. Grandma Didn't Wave Back by Rose Blue
      Debbie has always loved having Grandma live with
      them, but now Grandma is talking and acting strangely,
      as if she's a young girl again. Name this book.
      Debbie hoped Grandma's forgetfulness would get
      better, but one night a friend finds Grandma wandering
      outside in her nightgown. What is the title of this book?

365. Toliver's Secret by Esther Wood Brady
      Name the book in which Ellen has to smuggle a mes-
      sage, hidden inside a loaf of bread, to George Washing-
      ton.
      The British soldier wants to eat Ellen's loaf of bread
      but she is willing to fight rather than let him eat the
      bread in this book called....

366. The Murder of Hound Dog Bates by Robbie Branscum
      Sassafras thinks one of his three aunts poisoned his
      dog. Name the book in which he worries that the guilty
      aunt might poison him next.
      Sassafras Bates is sure either Aunt Veela, Aunt Hope
      or Aunt Faith killed his beloved dog and he aims to find
      out which one did it. Can you name that book?

367. All the Money in the World by Bill Brittain
      In what book will you find these things: a boy
      named Quentin, a little green man named Flan, three
      wishes and lots of money?
      Even the U.S. Army arrives when Quentin comes
      into a very large amount of money! Name that book!

368. The Wish Giver: Three Tales of Coven Tree by Bill
      Brittain
      Only four people at the annual Coven Tree Church
      Social are curious or brave enough to enter the tent
      of Thaddeus Blinn (whose eyes sometimes glow). In
      what book is each of the four given a white card with
      a red dot that places the forces of the universe at its
      owner's command?
      Polly Kemp starts to croak like a frog and a traveling
      salesman turns into a tree. In what book do these and
      other mysterious things happen in Coven Tree after
      Thaddeus Blinn passes through?

369. Trouble River by Betsy Byars
      The river is dangerous, but not as dangerous as an

Indian attack, so Dewey and his grandmother decide to
risk a river raft escape. This book is called....
    In this book Dewey's Grandma gets one of her scared
feelings, which usually means danger. Sure enough,
Dewey discovers an Indian lurking outside their cabin.
Name that book!

370. The TV Kid by Betsy Byars
      In what book does a boy named Lennie want to sub-
stitute an Armour Hot Dog jingle for learning a poem in
class at school?
      Lennie fantasizes that he is a quiz show contestant
and for his zonk prize, he has to spend one night in
a haunted house. What book is this?

371. That Julia Redfern by Eleanor Cameron
      In what book does a girl named Julia receive a mes-
sage from her dead father while she is unconscious after
a playground accident?
      Julia can get into trouble as easily as breathing.
She always comes out on top ... except when she is
knocked unconscious in a playground accident and
awakens to discover that she is locked in a strange
house with a weird old lady who won't let her out.
Name that book!

372. The Family Under the Bridge by Natalie Savage Carlson
      Armand, an old hobo in Paris, doesn't like children
because children mean responsibility and regular work,
two things he can do without. What book is he in?
      Name the book in which the three Calcet children ask
Father Christmas for a house on wheels, just like the
gypsies have.

373. My Brother Stevie by Eleanor Clymer
      In this book about two children living with their
grandmother in New York City, eight-year-old Stevie
Jenner has begun throwing rocks at trains and break-
ing into candy machines. Can you name it?
      Annie's only hope for keeping her little brother out
of trouble is his new teacher, Miss Stover, and the
teacher's dog, Skipper. In what book does Stevie's
behavior get worse when Miss Stover leaves school?

374. The Cat Who Went to Heaven by Elizabeth Coatsworth
      In this book the housekeeper of a penniless artist

goes out to find food, but instead brings back a three-
colored cat. What is the title?
    In which book does a faithful cat stand watch as an
old Japanese artist paints the death of Buddha for the
temple?

375. Sadako and the Thousand Paper Cranes by Eleanor
Coerr
    You can see how some Japanese people were hurt by
the atomic bomb because they have scars, but Sadako's
hurt can't be seen, even though it is deadly. Can you
name this book?
    Name the book in which a sick Japanese girl tries to
make her wish come true by folding birds out of paper.

376. The Matchlock Gun by Walter Edmonds
    This story tells of a Dutch family in New York colony.
When his father goes away, Edward is left to protect his
little sister, Trudy, and his mother. Name that book!
    In what book does Edward fire a gun loaded with
nails, buttons, and pins to protect his family from Indians?

377. Seeing Summer by Jeannette Eyerly
    Can you name the book in which Carrie Cramer's
excitement about a new neighbor girl turns into disap-
pointment when she learns that the new girl is blind?
    When Carrie Cramer first meets Jenny, she is sur-
prised that Jenny can do things like walk through a
room or make pudding. Name the book in which Carrie expects Jenny to be helpless because Jenny is blind.

378. Can't Catch Me, I'm the Gingerbread Man by Jamie Gilson
    In what book will you find such things as, "Toad in
the Hole," "Hot Dilly Dog Buns" and "Health Nutty Gingerbread"?
    In what book is Mitch McDandel the youngest contes-
tant in the Tenth ABC Bakeathon?

379. Harvey, the Beer Can King by Jamie Gilson
    Name the book in which Harvey Trumble gets egg-
bombed by Billy and Simon, two third graders he cheated
on a beer-can swap.
    Who will win the Superkid Contest--Suzanna and her
unicycle, Quint and his magic act, Eric and his skate-

board stunts or Harvey and his unusual collection?
Name this book.

380. Misty and Me by Barbara Girion
Kim isn't sure she likes her best friend, Lisa, any-
more. All Lisa is interested in these days is boys, but
Kim is more interested in getting a puppy. Can you
name that book?
Kim and her little brother Willie share a secret that
they must keep from their parents. The secret is that
they have a puppy but it lives at Mrs. Macvey's house.
Can you name this book?

381. The Mariah Delany Lending Library Disaster by Sheila
Greenwald
All the Delanys love to read except Mariah, but she
decides she loves books too when she hits upon the idea
of opening her own library. Name this funny story.
Name the book which tells about Mariah, a sixth-
grader who goes into competition with the New York
Public Library.

382. Time's Up by Florence Parry Heide
Noah's dad is an efficiency expert who likes to tell
people the most efficient way to do everything. He is
also a terrible cook, so Noah is delighted that his dad
is going on a business trip in this book called....
Noah's mother asks him to mail a letter. After getting the letter soaking wet, he puts it in the toaster
oven to dry out. After it burns, he destroys the evi-
dence in the garbage disposal. In what book does he
discover that he has destroyed a very important letter?

383. Long Claws; An Arctic Adventure by James Houston
In what book does a brave Eskimo girl named Upik
save her brother's life by throwing a piece of frozen
trout at a huge, hungry grizzly bear?
Upik and Pitohok think their troubles are over when
they find the frozen caribou to take to their starving
family, but as they begin their journey home they realize something is following them in this book called....

384. The Rabbi's Girls by Johanna Hurwitz
Carrie thinks she has found a friend in Selena Edwards, until Selena's grandmother calls her a "dirty Jew"

and forbids Selena to play with Carrie. What book is
this?

Name the book in which two sisters, Carrie and
Doris, enter a coloring contest because they want to
win tickets to the circus.

385. The Animal Family by Randall Jarrell
In what book do a lonely hunter and a mermaid live
together happily in a house by the sea?
This family consists of a hunter, a mermaid, a bear,
a lynx and a boy. Name their story.

386. No Beasts! No Children! by Beverly Keller
In this book a woman wants to pay Anthony two
hundred dollars for his doll, Poor Thing, but he trades
it for a mouse. What is the title?

In what book will you find the twins, Aida and Anthony, who won't talk to anyone except ruffians, dere-
licts and each other?

387. Hocus-Pocus Dilemma by Pat Kibbe
Name the book in which B.J. Pinkerton goes into the
fortune-telling business after she decides she must have
ESP.

B.J.'s brother, Ethan, gets a big surprise when he
discovers something other than a raccoon in his raccoon
trap! This funny story is called....

388. Jennifer, Hecate, Macbeth, William McKinley, and Me,
Elizabeth by E.L. Konigsburg
In order to become a witch, Elizabeth is willing to do
the things Jennifer says, like eat raw eggs and drink
lion's milk, but she refuses to kill a frog named Hilary
Ezra. Name that book!

In which book does Elizabeth's onion breath nearly
blow Cynthia away during rehearsals for the Christmas
play?

389. The Fledgling by Jane Langton
Georgie wants to fly. In what book does the Goose
Prince teach her how?

Every night Georgie sneaks out of the house and
flies with the Goose Prince and every night her mother
lies awake waiting for her safe return in this book
called....

390. Rabbit Hill by Robert Lawson
        Running for his life, Little Georgie is sure he has
left the hound dog far behind, then he realizes he is
trapped by Deadman's Brook. What is the title?
        In what book does Father hop right out in front of
the New Folks' moving car to see if they have good
manners?

391. Pippi Longstocking by Astrid Lindgren
        This is the first book about a nine-year-old girl
with hair the color of a carrot, a blue dress with red
patches, one brown and one black stocking, and a pair
of black shoes exactly twice as long as her feet. Can
you name it?
        When this redhead comes upon five big bullies beat-
ing up little Willie, she picks them up and hangs them
over branches and gateposts and throws one right over
the fence. What is the title?

392. Joel and the Great Merlini by Eloise Jarvis McGraw
        At first Joel Penny likes his unusual friend who
helps him do magic tricks, but now he wishes he would
just disappear in this book called....
        What boy do you know who can change nickels to
quarters, rocks to skate-boards, and flowers to fire-
crackers? Joel, that's who. What book is he in?

393. Judge Benjamin: Superdog by Judith Whitelock McIner-
ney
        This huge St. Bernard dog is the guardian of his
human family and he doesn't want to share them with
anyone, especially General Henry. What book is this?
        To keep them out of trouble, the O'Riley family locks
the two dogs in the garage while they're out shopping.
The dogs accidentally turn the water spigot on and
can't shut it off. In what book does a wall of water
greet the family when they open the garage door?

394. Mr. Little by Robert Newton Peck
        In what book do Drag and Finley plant a copy of
"Hotsy Harem" magazine inside their new teacher's umbrella?
        Drag and Finley looked forward to having Miss Kel-
log for their teacher when school started. Instead they
end up with a new man teacher who knows how to dish
out tricks as well as take them. What book is this?

395. Soup by Robert Newton Peck
    One broken window in the Baptist Church leads to
another, and before you know it, old Mrs. Stetson and
Rob are running for cover! Name that book!
    In what book do Rob and his best friend hide a stone
in their ball of tinfoil to get extra money from Mr. Dis-
kin at the junkyard?

396. Soup on Wheels by Robert Newton Peck
    These two best friends from Miss Kelly's class are
always getting into trouble. In what book does their
decision to enter the Children's Costume Contest dressed
as a zebra on roller skates lead to disaster?
    What book has a character named Beverly Bean?
Clue: Beverly is a new boy in Miss Kelly's class, and
he immediately moves in on Rob's girlfriend, Norma Jean
Bissell.

397. Betsy's Up-and-Down Year by Anne Pellowski
    Betsy Korb just can't keep track of her retainer.
In this book it is thrown away during a picnic, lost in
a batch of taffy and chewed up by a tiny dog. What is
the title of her story?
    When Betsy Korb gets her ankle caught in a fence,
a buffalo begins to lick her foot. Name that book!

398. Willow Wind Farm: Betsy's Story by Anne Pellowski
    This big farm family has ten children. Their favorite
family stories are the ones about how grandma lost the
tip of one finger and how grandpa shook hands with a
bear. Can you name this book?
    In what book does a little girl get lost while playing
flashlight tag because she hides in a laundry basket
and falls asleep? Clue: Her name is Kristine Korb and
she is the youngest of ten children.

399. The Hoboken Chicken Emergency by Daniel Manus Pink-
    water
    Arthur Bobowitz can't find a turkey for Thanksgiving,
but he finds something even better, or at least bigger,
in this book entitled....
    Name the book in which one of the main characters
is a 226-pound chicken named Henrietta.

400. The Best Christmas Pageant Ever by Barbara Robinson
    This family lives over a garage; a "beware of the

cat" sign is in their yard, and their last name is Herd-
man. What book are they in?
    Name the book in which Claude Herdman wrecks his
first-grade classroom by bringing his one-eyed, angry
(because it hasn't been fed for two days) cat to school
for show and tell.

401. How to Eat Fried Worms by Thomas Rockwell
        Butter-and-fried-worm sandwich, whizbang worm de-
    light, worm and egg on rye, ketchup-covered worm--
    in what book do you find all these dishes?
        Will Billy win the $50.00 bet he made with Alan?
    All he has to do is eat a disgusting, crawly worm every
    day for fifteen days in this book called....

402. Goodbye My Island by Jean Rogers
        Every year the U.S. Navy icebreaker comes to King
    Island, and every year after their visit most of the
    Eskimos get sick from the germs the sailors carry. This
    book is called....
        All summer the Eskimo girl Esther Atoolik and her
    family live in Nome. In the fall they return to their
    true home in this book called....

403. Blind Outlaw by Glen Rounds
        This boy makes chirping noises to animals because
    he cannot speak, but he communicates better than any-
    one else to a blind horse in this book called....
        The boy couldn't speak but animals loved him and
    followed him around. He was even able to pull porcu-
    pine quills out of the vicious ranch dog. What is the
    name of this book?

404. Chester Cricket's New Home by George Selden
        Name the book in which Chester Cricket has to move
    because his tree stump home was destroyed when two
    fat women sat on it.
        Can you name the book in which Chester Cricket
    finds that he has many friends who are willing to let
    him live with them after his home is destroyed?

405. The Cricket in Times Square by George Selden
        In what book do Harry Cat and Tucker Mouse take
    their new friend from Connecticut on a tour of Times
    Square in New York City?

In what book does a cricket chirp Italian love songs
to keep Mama Bellini from throwing him out of the news-
stand?

406. Harry Cat's Pet Puppy by George Selden
In what book does Harry Cat bring home what Tucker
Mouse at first thinks is a dirty dish mop?
Harry and Tucker face a big problem--Huppy has
grown too big to fit in their drainpipe home. Name that
book!

407. Mysteriously Yours, Maggie Marmelstein by Marjorie
Sharmat
Maggie sneaks something to Noah by trading lunches
with him. Her lunch always has something horrible in
it, like liver crackers, so that only Noah will want to
swap with her. Name that book!
Every student in school wants to be the Mystery
Person, who writes articles for the school newspaper.
Name the book in which a girl named Maggie gets the
honor and a lot of problems.

408. Getting Something on Maggie Marmelstein by Marjorie
Sharmat
In what book does Maggie threaten to tell every kid
in school that Thad is a sissy cook because he helped
her mother make bread pudding?
So Thad can get revenge on someone who is spread-
ing stories about him, he takes the role of a frog in
the class play. Name the book.

409. Mr. Wolf and Me by Mary Francis Shura
A Halloween prank, letting all the animals at the
vet's kennel loose, may cost Miles' dog his life in this
book called....
Something is killing farmer Agger's sheep. He thinks
it is Miles' German Shepherd and he wants the dog
destroyed! Name that book!

410. Einstein Anderson Makes Up for Lost Time by Seymour
Simon
Name the book in which Einstein Anderson comes up
with an idea called the Booth of the Impossible Trick
for his school fair.
In this book Einstein Anderson proves that Pat the

Brat Burns is lying when he claims to have thrown pea-
nut butter and jelly sandwiches at a snake. What is
its title?

411. The Fearsome Inn by Isaac Bashevis Singer
     Name the book in which Leibel's magic chalk traps
Doboshova the witch and her husband in the kitchen of
their inn.
     In what book does Leibel, a student of the cabala,
the ancient Hebrew books, make a devil and a witch
sign an oath in their own blood?

412. A Taste of Blackberries by Doris Buchanan Smith
     When Jamie gets stung by bees, his friend thinks
he is showing off by rolling around on the ground--
until the ambulance arrives. Name that book!
     What do you do when your best friend dies? Espe-
cially when your best friend is Jamie, the clown, the
show-off, the crazy best friend who pokes a stick down
a bee hole and dies because of it. Name his story.

413. Abel's Island by William Steig
     Name the book in which a very fashionable mouse
named Abelard Hassam di Chirico Flint from Mossville
finds himself marooned in the top of a tree by a very
rude hurricane.
     In this book a mouse tries to cross a river by raft,
sailboat, rowboat, crabgrass rope, stepping stones and
even by trying to catapult himself across. What is the
title?

414. Cat Walk by Mary Stolz
     Roddy throws a cat against a tractor, then kicks it
into a telephone booth. Finally, his father arrives and
stops him from hurting the cat again in this book
called....
     Against his mother's advice, this wild barn cat wants
to have a name and to be someone's pet. In a few
months he has had more owners and more names than
he can remember. What is the title?

415. When Grandfather Journeys into Winter by Craig Strete
     The prize for riding the unbroken horse Rolling
Thunder is $500.00, but if Tayhua wins, he wants the
horse, not the money. What book is he in?

Rolling Thunder bucks so hard that blood bursts from Tayhua's nose but he won't fall off because he's determined to win the horse for his grandson in this book called....

416. Mary Poppins by P.L. Travers
When their new nanny first comes to Number 17 Cherry Tree Lane, Jane and Michael notice that she slides up the bannister! What book is this?

This English nanny takes a bottle of marvelous medicine from her empty carpet bag, that tastes like strawberry ice and lime cordial to Michael and Jane, milk to the twins, and rum punch to herself. Name her story.

417. The Great Christmas Kidnapping Caper by Jean Van Leeuwen
The headline reads, "Santa Claus Missing." In what book do Marvin, Fats, and Raymond discover where Santa can be found?

Name the book in which the Santa Claus at Gimbel's department store kidnaps the Macy's department-store Santa.

418. The Great Rescue Operation by Jean Van Leeuwen
Fats, a mouse that lives in Macy's, loves sweets but most of all he loves dill pickles. Name the book in which he leaves Macy's because a doll house is purchased for a lonely little girl.

Fats is missing. Raymond and Marvin are determined to find him, even though it means the two tiny mice have to leave their home in Macy's and ride the subway across New York City. Can you name that book?

419. Hawkins by Barbara Brooks Wallace
When ten-year-old Harvey finds a torn coupon for a free thing, he sends it in and gets back a real-live gentleman's gentleman to serve him for a month. Name that book!

Not used to undressing in front of anyone, Harvey hides in the closet and accidentally knocks over his ant farm, which breaks into pieces. This funny book is called....

420. Hawkins and the Soccer Solution by Barbara Brooks Wallace

In which book does Harvey's soccer team change
names from Mike's Bikes to Doody's Doobies?
   In what book do Harvey and Woodie bake a Soup-er
Bean Cheese Pickle Chip Cake to raise money to buy
soccer uniforms?

421. Charlotte's Web by E.B. White
      In what book will you meet Charlotte A. Cavatica, a
spider, Wilbur the pig, Templeton the rat, and Fern
Arable, the girl who could understand their language?
      This little pig has a blood-drinking friend who saves
his life before she dies. Name that book!

422. The Trumpet of the Swan by E.B. White
      In what book does Sam make friends with a family
of swans by saving them from a hungry fox?
      Louis is a good swimmer and flyer but he cannot
make a sound, which is a great disadvantage for a
trumpeter swan. Can you name his story?

423. The First Four Years by Laura Ingalls Wilder
      What book tells of the birth of Rose, Laura and Al-
manzo's daughter, on the Dakota prairie in the 1880's?
      In this book Laura and Almanzo get married quickly
so Almanzo's family won't insist on a big church wedding.
Can you name it?

424. A Visit to William Blake's Inn by Nancy Willard
      Which book of poetry features an inn where the
bakers are two mighty dragons?
      In what poetry book do sunflowers ask the innkeeper
for a room with a view?

                        ADVANCED READING

425. Get Lost, Little Brother by Carole S. Adler
      Because Todd won't open the door and share the
bathroom with his twin brothers, they wedge the door
shut. Can you name the book in which Todd is trapped
inside the bathroom all day?
      Todd has always had trouble making friends. Name
the book in which an island helps Todd become friends
with two misfits, Louie, a girl who's always in trouble

at school, and Hank, a foster child who's been taken
from his parents because he can't stop stealing.

426. Searching for Shona by Margaret J. Anderson
    In what book do Marjorie Malcolm-Scott and Shona
    McInnes exchange identities when they are being evacu-
    ated from Edinburgh?
    Name the book in which a wealthy Scottish girl trades
    places with an adventurous orphan during World War II.

427. Emily Upham's Revenge by Avi
    Name the book in which Seth tries to talk little Emily
    into lying down on the railroad tracks to stop the train
    so that they can ask the conductor how much a ticket
    to Boston costs.
    In what book is seven-year-old Emily Octavia Upham
    left at the mercy of Deadwood Dick when her uncle fails
    to meet her at the train station?

428. Eyes of the Amaryllis by Natalie Babbitt
    Name the book in which the ghost of Stewart Reade
    is doomed to walk the shore at high tide looking for
    treasures that the sea might want returned to its watery
    depths.
    Can you name the book in which the sea creates a
    terrible storm to force Jenny and her grandmother to
    return a wooden head that has washed ashore?

429. The Search for Delicious by Natalie Babbitt
    Twelve-year-old Gaylen is sent on a very important
    errand--to poll the kingdom over which food should stand
    for "Delicious" in the new dictionary. In what book
    does this happen?
    Name the book that has 900-year-old woldwellers who
    live in the treetops, dwarves, a mermaid, and a king-
    dom about to be split by civil war--all because of a
    dictionary.

430. Miss Hickory by Carolyn S. Bailey
    When this lady's house is taken over by a chipmunk,
    she almost freezes to death until Crow comes to her
    rescue. Name that book!
    This doll is afraid she might lose her head if her
    neighbor gets hungry. He is a squirrel and her head
    is a nut. Can you name her story?

431. <u>Are You There God? It's Me, Margaret</u> by Judy Blume
      When Margaret moves to New Jersey, she gets to join
      a secret club called the Four PTS's. What book is this?
      Because she has no religion, Margaret goes to temple
      with her grandmother and to church with her friend
      Janie so she can find out whether she should join the
      Y or the Jewish Community Center. Name her story.

432. <u>Blubber</u> by Judy Blume
      When chubby Linda gives a report on whales, Jill
      joins the crowd in giving her an insulting nickname.
      What is the title of this book?
      Name the book in which Jill and Tracy break rotten
      eggs in Mr. Machinist's mailbox on Halloween.

433. <u>The Toad on Capitol Hill</u> by Esther Wood Brady
      When Dorsy jumps down from a tree, her yellow
      dress gets caught on a limb and is pulled back over
      her head, leaving her looking like a peeled banana.
      Can you name that book?
      In what book does Dorsy McCurdy make a wish on
      a white toad? The wish is that her stepfamily, the
      Trowbridges, will move back to Philadelphia.

434. <u>The Bad Times of Irma Baumlein</u> by Carol Ryrie Brink
      Irma is sorry that Bob Hickey is in trouble because
      she stole the biggest doll in the world, so she hits him
      on the head with a purse full of money! Name that
      book!
      Judy gives Irma a hamster in the hopes that Irma
      will show her the biggest doll in the world. What book
      are they in?

435. <u>Christmas with Ida Early</u> by Robert Burch
      The twins Clay and Dewey try to make the new
      preacher think that their housekeeper is in love with
      him by putting tiny paper hearts on his dinner plate,
      but instead of thinking the housekeeper put them there,
      he eats them! Name that book!
      The main character in this book has a way with an-
      imals. She's the only one who can get a stubborn don-
      key to perform in Brother Preston's Christmas Tableau,
      but he's forbidden her to attend because she yodels
      when the choir sings. Can you name that book?

436. Ida Early Comes over the Mountain by Robert Burch
        Life is never quite the same for the Sutton family
      after Ida Early comes to keep house for them in this
      book called....
        Name the book in which Ida Early gives the Sutton
      twins, Clay and Dewey, a bath with all their clothes
      on.

437. Queenie Peavy by Robert Burch
        In what book does Queenie set a trap for Cravey
      Mason because he has teased her about her father being
      in the penitentiary?
        This girl has a deadly aim, whether it is spitting
      tobacco at the coal stove in the courtroom or throwing
      a stone at a squirrel sixty feet away. Name the book
      in which she is accused of breaking the church windows.

438. The Incredible Journey by Sheila Burnford
        Half of a scribbled note, accidentally burned in the
      fireplace, marks the beginning of an unbelievable trip
      by three animal friends. What is the title of this book?
        When the dam broke, Tao, a cat, and Luath, a dog,
      were caught midstream by a torrent of water. Name
      that book!

439. After the Goat Man by Betsy Byars
        Harold and Ada go with Figgy to see Figgy's grand-
      father. The grandfather has barricaded himself in his
      cabin with a gun and has threatened to shoot anyone
      who comes near. This book is called....
        Overweight Harold has imagined himself as many
      things--a cowboy, a baseball player, and an astronaut--
      but never as a brave hero, until the day that Harold
      must stop Figgy's grandfather from shooting someone.
      Name that book!

440. The Cartoonist by Betsy Byars
        The most important thing in Alfie's life is drawing
      comic strips, and the only place he can draw them is in
      his own special attic. In which book is Alfie afraid his
      attic is going to be taken from him?
        His mother wants him to be a football player; his
      grandfather wants him to build cars, but Alfie's dream-
      world is one of cartoons. What book is he in?

441. The Glory Girl by Betsy Byars
      The Glory twins, Joshua and Matthew, have an on-
going competition to see who can collect the most stitches.
For a while they are almost even, forty-nine to forty-
two. Then in one unbelievable bicycle accident, Joshua's
tally jumps up to ninety-one! Name that book!
      The Glory family are gospel singers and they try
very hard to be good law-abiding Christians. Therefore they are not at all happy that Uncle Newt, the
bank robber, is out of prison and coming to live with
them. Can you name this book?

442. The Wonderful Flight to the Mushroom Planet by Eleanor
      Cameron
      Name the book in which two boys set off in a home-
made rocket ship to the planet Basidium.
      In which book does a strange little scientist put an
ad in the paper for a small spaceship built by one or
two boys?

443. Fritzi's Winter by John W. Chambers
      When Fritzi, the Siamese cat, accidentally gets left
behind on Fire Island, she must learn to fend for herself, something she has never had to do before. This
book is called....
      For the first time in her life, the cat Fritzi must
learn to find her own food and save herself from ene-
mies, such as the cold snow and a fox that chases her
out on a limb. Name that book!

444. Barney and the UFO by Margaret Goff Clark
      Is Tibbo the space boy really a friend? Barney
finds out when he changes his mind about going home
with him. Can you name the title of this book?
      Barney is convinced his foster parents are going to
send him back to the orphanage, so he accepts an invitation from a visitor from outer space. What is the title
of this book?

445. Ellen Grae by Vera and Bill Cleaver
      Can you name the eleven-year-old girl who takes off
her petticoat and stuffs it into her desk everyday when
she gets to school? Her name is the title of the book.
      In what book does a treasure hunt lead Ira, Ellen
Grae, Grover, and Missouri to a double grave in the
middle of a swamp?

446. Grover by Vera and Bill Cleaver
       Barefoot and in his old clothes, this boy lands a job
       he didn't even want--delivering telegrams--thanks to his
       friend, Ellen Grae. Name that book!
       In what book do Ellen Grae, Grover, and Ferrell
       sneak up a hill at dawn to capture a turkey and get
       revenge on mean Betty Repkin?

447. The Curse of Camp Gray Owl by Patricia Edwards Clyne
       Chad is about to lose his grip on the tree limb and
       plunge twenty feet onto sharp rocks, when someone or
       something helps him in this book called....
       Roy's friends are determined to find some way to con-
       vince him to return to school, even if it means risking
       an Indian curse! Name that book!

448. Felicia the Critic by Ellen Conford
       Because of her criticisms, this girl causes a traffic
       jam in front of her school, almost gets her family thrown
       out of a restaurant, and ruins a wedding. Name that
       book!
       In order to join a club, this girl has to promise to
       keep her mouth shut and not criticize anything that goes
       on at the meetings. She is sure that the other members
       are making plans for a project that will lead to disaster,
       but she can't say anything. Name that book.

449. Dorp Dead by Julia Cunningham
       Gilly Ground's foster parent has a dog named Mash
       that he keeps in a wooden cage and beats until it bleeds.
       One night Gilly discovers that another cage is being
       built for Gilly himself. Name that book!
       The orphanage is so noisy that Gilly is happy to go
       to a foster home, until he discovers that his foster
       parent, Mr. Kobalt, is insane and has something very
       unpleasant planned for him. What book is Gilly in?

450. The BFG by Roald Dahl
       What book has Childchewer, Maidmasher, Bonecrusher,
       Gizzardgulper and five other giants, all of whom like
       to eat "human beans?"
       If any "human bean" ever sees a giant, he or she
       must be taken away so that other "human beans" won't
       start hunting giants. In what book is Sophie taken
       away?

451. Charlie and the Chocolate Factory by Roald Dahl
          What book has the following characters: Augustus
      Gloop, Veruca Salt, Violet Beauregarde, Mike Teavee,
      and Charlie Bucket? They are the lucky five with golden
      tickets to visit a very special place.
          In what book does Grandpa Joe, who has been in
      bed for twenty years, dance for joy in his pajamas--all
      because of a candy bar?

452. Charlie and the Great Glass Elevator by Roald Dahl
          In what book does Grandma Josephine take four
      tablets that make her go backward in time until she is
      just a little baby?
          In what book do Charlie Bucket and his companions
      find themselves caught between Space Hotel U.S.A. and
      a huge Commuter Capsule?

453. Danny, the Champion of the World by Roald Dahl
          In what book does nine-year-old Danny set out alone
      in the middle of the night, driving a Baby Austin to
      find his father?
          In what book will you find out about several ways
      to poach a pheasant, including "The Horsehair Stop-
      per," "The Sticky Hat," and best of all, "The Sleeping
      Beauty"?

454. James and the Giant Peach by Roald Dahl
          In what book do a boy and several strange creatures
      like a centipede with boots and a spider travel to the
      other side of the ocean inside a fruit?
          Because James spills the bag, the one thousand
      crocodile tongues, boiled in the skull of a dead witch,
      work their magic on a fruit tree instead of on him.
      What book is he in?

455. Zucchini by Barbara Dana
          In what book will you meet Billy who is so shy he
      rarely speaks, and a ferret whose name is the title of
      this book?
          A tiny ferret escapes from the New York City ASPCA
      and travels by himself to the prairies of Oklahoma. Can
      you name his story?

456. Nothing's Fair in Fifth Grade by Barthe De Clements
          Elsie's skirt falls off in front of her entire fifth

grade class because she has finally lost some weight.
Name that book!

Convinced that the truck driver is trying to kidnap
them, the fifth graders jump off his truck at the first
red light, but Elsie's little sister doesn't jump. In what
book do they watch in horror as she is driven away?

457. Along Came a Dog by Meindert DeJong
Every time the farmer drops the big black dog far
from the farm, the dog finds his way back. In what
book is the dog's only friend a little red hen?

Name the book in which a big black dog is perfectly
happy to be bossed around by a little red hen who
doesn't realize she is supposed to be an outcast?

458. Hurry Home, Candy by Meindert DeJong
Because of his fear of a broom, a little dog is left
behind in a thunderstorm and is soon lost in the countryside. What is the name of his story?

In what book does a pack of dogs attack a starving
puppy when he races to pick up a dead chicken on the
road?

459. Shadrach by Meindert DeJong
Davie's little black rabbit has a name right out of
the Bible. His name is the title of this book. Do you
know it?

After being sick for so long, Davie sneaks out of
his bed two days in a row to get everything ready for
his rabbit, and his big brother lies to keep him out of
trouble. Name his story.

460. The Champion of Merrimack County by Roger W. Drury
In what book will you find a mouse named O Crispin,
who likes to race his bike around the rim of Mr. Berryfield's bathtub?

The search for a new bicycle wheel leads Janet
Berryfield from the bicycle shop to the clockmaker, to
the blacksmith, and finally to the dentist. Give the
title of this funny book.

461. Susannah and the Blue House Mystery by Patricia El-
more
In what book does Susannah discover where Mr.
Withers hid something valuable by looking in a book
entitled HISTORICAL MANSIONS OF CROATIA?

Name the book in which Lucy, Susannah, and Knievel Jones sneak into an old house to solve a mystery.

462. Thimble Summer by Elizabeth Enright
Garnet's first night ever spent away from home becomes more exciting when a strange boy appears to beg some coffee. What book is this?
In what book does nine-year-old Garnet Linden have to hitchhike home because she spends all her money on presents?

463. Ginger Pye by Eleanor Estes
Dusting pews in church can be fun, Rachel and Jerry discover, if you tie the duster on your baby uncle and send him sliding back and forth. Name that book!
In which book are Jerry and Rachel Pye followed by a mysterious figure in a yellow hat?

464. Chitty-Chitty-Bang-Bang by Ian Fleming
The big green Paragon Panther belonged to the Pott family, and was not only a car, but also a boat and an airplane. What is the title of its story?
When Joe the Monster and his gang take after the Pott family, the Potts' only hope is their car. Name it and you will have the title of the book.

465. The Great Bamboozlement by Jane Flory
A few tree branches are the only things keeping the Dowell family and their floating store from being destroyed in the flooded river! Name that book!
Owning a store that floats on a raft causes the Dowell family to become involved in many adventures. Name the book where they encounter floods, bank robbers, mean ring-tailed roarers, and a runaway.

466. Between Friends by Sheila Garrigue
Jill's mother doesn't seem happy about Dede Atkins, the first friend Jill makes in York Falls. Dede is retarded. Name that book!
To get retarded Dede to stop crying, Jill promises her an invitation to a birthday party she's not even having. What is the title of the book?

467. <u>The Gift of the Pirate Queen</u> by Patricia Reilly Giff
    Grace's mother died a year ago, so Cousin Fiona
Tierney is coming from Ireland to take care of Grace
and her sister Amy. Name the book in which Grace
hates Fiona, sight unseen, because she thinks Fiona
is trying to take her mother's place.
    Amy won't behave. Even though she is diabetic she
won't follow her diet and eat correctly. Now she is unconscious on top of the fire tower and Grace can't carry
her down again. Name that book!

468. <u>Philip Hall Likes Me, I Reckon Maybe</u> by Bette Greene
    Eleven-year-old Beth Lambert is only second-best in
arithmetic, spelling and reading in Miss Johnson's class
--and all because of a boy she likes. Name that book!
    The cutest boy in J.T. Williams School and the brav-
est Tiger Hunter is Beth Lambert's good friend ... or
is he? What book is this?

469. <u>Al(exandra) the Great</u> by Constance C. Greene
    Al wants to have hair like the girls in TV commer-
cials, hair that bounces and shines, but that's okay,
since Al is a girl, in this book called....
    Al is really looking forward to spending the summer
in the country with her father and stepmother because
she will get to see Brian, but something happens to her
mother that may cancel her trip! Name that book!

470. <u>Ask Anybody</u> by Constance C. Greene
    Schuyler Sweet's friend Nell, who is too young to
have a driver's license, decides to drive her Uncle Joe's
truck. In what book does she run over the family's
dog?
    Name the book in which Sidney flushes his brother
Tad's tooth down the toilet because he doesn't want the
tooth fairy sneaking into their room at night.

471. <u>I and Sproggy</u> by Constance C. Greene
    Adam's father tells him to look after his new English
stepsister, but on their first outing together she saves
him from a mugger! Name that book!
    Adam doesn't want a stepsister, and when one is
forced on him he fights back. In what book is he so
mean to Sproggy, his stepsister, that she cries and even
his friends think he is rotten?

472. The Unmaking of Rabbit by Constance C. Greene
      Eugene's advice to Rabbit is to act like you have to
      throw up if you ever get into a bad scene and want to
      leave it quickly. What book are they in?
      Freddy and his gang are planning a caper. They
      want to rob from the rich and give to the poor--them-
      selves. Can you name the book where they will let
      Paul in on the caper if he doesn't chicken out?

473. All the Way to Wit's End by Sheila Greenwald
      Drucilla Brattles has the Bundage mouth. It makes
      her look like Bugs Bunny, so she wants to get rid of
      it. What book is she in?
      Name the book in which Drucilla Brattles holds a
      garage sale to earn money for braces.

474. Max and Me and the Time Machine by Gery Greer and
      Bob Ruddick
      For only two dollars and fifty cents, Steve and Max
      buy themselves a trip to thirteenth-century England.
      Steve thinks the time-travel trip is great because he
      becomes Sir Robert, the brave knight, but Max isn't
      very happy because he becomes Sir Robert's horse!
      Name that book!
      Steve thinks three measly hours isn't enough time to
      spend in medieval England, so when Max isn't looking he
      moves the time machine's dial forward three notches, to
      what he thinks is eight hours. What book is this?

475. Taffy Sinclair Strikes Again by Betsy Haynes
      Name the book in which Jana Morgan learns all about
      body language from a classmate named Taffy.
      Jana and her friends think wearing their Fabulous
      Five T-shirts to school is a good idea, until they re-
      member Miss Wiggins, their sixth-grade teacher. Name
      that book.

476. Banana Blitz by Florence Parry Heide
      Jonah's nickname at Fairlee School is "Fish." That's
      what he and his room smell like, thanks to Goober's
      habit of eating fish because he thinks it's brain food.
      Name that book!
      Arriving at Fairlee School, Jonah finds that his room-
      mate, Goober, is now into eating fish. He has stocked
      their room's refrigerator with sardines and there's no
      room for Jonah's candy bars! What book are they in?

477. Banana Twist by Florence Parry Heide
     Name the book in which Jonah Krock tries to help
     Goober Grube save the lives of a bunch of bananas.
     What book introduces a character named Goober, who
     has lots of pimples, an aquarium and loves banana splits
     with peanuts?

478. Justin Morgan Had a Horse by Marguerite Henry
     In what book does a Vermont schoolmaster get two
     colts instead of money as payment from Farmer Beane?
     What book tells the story of Joel Goss, who works
     as an apprentice in a sawmill during the day, goes to
     school at night, and after that, tames a colt for his
     schoolmaster?

479. King of the Wind by Marguerite Henry
     Even though the mare has died, her colt survives
     on camel's milk and wild honey, thanks to Agba, a
     small stable-boy. Name that book!
     Name the book in which you will meet Agba, a mute
     Moroccan stable-boy; Shams, a thoroughbred Arabian
     stallion; and Grimalkin, a faithful tomcat.

480. Misty of Chincoteague by Marguerite Henry
     Twenty Spanish ponies are on their way to work in
     the gold mines of Peru. In what book does a storm at
     sea give them freedom and an island of their own?
     No one has ever caught the Phantom before, but
     Paul and Maureen are determined that on Pony Penning
     Day she will be theirs. Name that book!

481. What If They Knew? by Patricia Hermes
     The entire fifth-grade class bursts into laughter
     when they meet their new teacher. She's huge, over
     six feet tall, with big feet and messy hair. Her name
     is Miss Gladstone and when she speaks, she squeaks
     like a cartoon character. What book is she in?
     No one in Miss Gladstone's fifth-grade class likes
     Carrie Wibler because she's a teacher's pet and a brat.
     So when she is chosen to give the speech for Parents'
     Night at school, the other girls plan their revenge. It
     has something to do with dead mice. Name that book!

482. Alvin's Swap Shop by Clifford Hicks
     The Pest and Shoie help Alvin start a great business

without any money at all, but they didn't plan on deal-
ing with a murderer! What book is this?
    Scarface is after the treasure. He has killed one
man for it and now he wants to kill Pim. This book is
called....

483. The Wacky World of Alvin Fernald by Clifford Hicks
    When this boy tugs on his right earlobe, you know
his magnificent brain is at work thinking up wacky
ideas. In what book does he think up an April Fool
joke that wins him the coveted Joker of the Year trophy?
    This boy builds his own flying machine from lumber,
a bicycle and his mother's living room drapes. Does
it fly? I hope so. He intends to try it by pedaling
off a cliff and the only parachute he has is an umbrella! Can you name this book?

484. Prisoners at the Kitchen Table by Barbara Holland
    Polly Conover is tough. She can run faster and hit
a ball harder than any boy in her class, but Josh Blake
sees her cry when they're kidnapped in this book
called....
    In what book are Polly and Josh forced to help their
kidnappers rob a store?

485. Tough Luck Karen by Johanna Hurwitz
    Karen is the only one at the Halloween Party without
a costume. Fortunately, another girl shares her costume, a king-size sheet, and she and Karen become Sia-
mese twin ghosts. Name that book!
    Karen's science project is very unusual. No student
has ever done one quite like it. In what book does her
science project make her very popular with her fellow
classmates? Clue: Her project is edible.

486. The Song in the Walnut Grove by David Kherdian
    Ben, an adventurous, world-exploring cricket, be-
comes friends with Charley, the grasshopper. Together
they outwit two boys who think the only thing to do
with grasshoppers and crickets is to squash them!
Name that book.
    Name the book in which Ben the cricket wants to do
more than chirrup at night, so he sets out to explore
the world in the daytime and is attacked by cricket-
hating grasshoppers.

487. The Jungle Book by Rudyard Kipling
       Name the book with these characters: Mowgli the
      man-cub, Shere Khan the tiger, Bagheera the black
      panther, and old Baloo the bear.
       In this book a boy's teachers are an old brown bear
      and a black panther. Together they teach him the ways
      of the jungle, but warn him that one day he must re-
      turn to the world of men. Name that book!

488. Big Red by Jim Kjelgaard
       Can a $7,000 show dog be a varmint dog too? Danny
      Pickett and his father find out in this book called....
       Name the book in which Danny Pickett, a poor young
      trapper, gets the chance to train a champion Irish Set-
      ter.

489. Calling B For Butterfly by Louise Lawrence
       Six out of 1200 people survive the asteroid's collision
      with the starliner Sky Rider, but the rescuer's compu-
      ters detect seven heart beats! Name that book!
       Four teenagers, a little girl, and a baby are the only
      human survivors of Sky Rider's collision with an asteroid,
      and none of them know how to operate the controls of
      the life ferry. This book is called....

490. Strawberry Girl by Lois Lenski
       In what book does Birdie Boyer introduce the Slater
      children for the first time in their lives to a comb and
      a mirror?
       If you want to know how sprinkling flour on straw-
      berry plants can keep them from getting trampled, read
      the book called....

491. The Voyages of Doctor Doolittle by Hugh Lofting
       Can you name the book about the adventures of a
      great naturalist who is busy learning the language of
      the shellfish and has a duck for a housekeeper?
       The crew of the Curlew consists of a famous natural-
      ist, his ten-year-old assistant, Bumpo the Crown Prince
      of Jolliginki, a dog, a monkey, and a parrot. In what
      book do they set off for Spidermonkey Island?

492. In the Year of the Boar and Jackie Robinson by Bette
      Bao Lord
       On her first day in America, Shirley Temple Wong

gets lost when she goes to the store to buy her father
cigarettes. She can't ask for help because she speaks
only Chinese. What book is she in?
   Name the book in which Mabel and Shirley Temple
Wong become friends, but only after Shirley refuses
to squeal on Mabel for giving her two black eyes.

493. The One Hundredth Thing About Caroline by Lois Lowry
      Caroline and her friend Stacy are convinced that
Frederick Fiske, the man living upstairs, is a poisoner.
Name the book in which Caroline is horrified when her
mother starts to date the man.
      Name the book in which Caroline deliberately pours
a glass of milk over a dinner guest's feet because she
wants him to take his shoes off.

494. Raising a Mother Isn't Easy by Elisabeth McHugh
      Karen decides that Marvin, her guinea pig, needs a
wife and that Barbara, her mother, needs a husband.
In what book does she try to find spouses for both of
them?
      Must like animals, must like to cook, must like to
read--these are part of Karen's list of attributes a man
must have in order to marry her mother. What book
is she in?

495. The Toothpaste Millionaire by Jean Merrill
      This book is about twelve-year-old Rufus Mayflower
and how he got to be a millionaire. Can you name it?
      If you want to know how to go into business and
make a big profit, read about Rufus Mayflower and Kate
MacKinstrey in this book entitled....

496. Blind Flight by Hilary Milton
      A wild goose crashes through the airplane's wind-
shield, leaving the pilot unconscious. Now Debbie must
pilot the plane, in this book called....
      In what book does a blind girl have to pilot an air-
plane by herself?

497. Something to Count On by Emily Moore
      In what book does Lorraine have to spend the day
in Miss Crane's fourth grade while the rest of Mr. Hamilton's fifth grade goes to the museum?

Lorraine and Jason's daddy says he loves them, but when it comes to keeping promises, he's too busy. Name the book in which, even though Lorraine is suspended from school, her father goes on vacation instead of meeting with her teacher.

498. The Borrowers by Mary Norton
Once you have been seen, it is time to emigrate out of the house--or else you might be eaten by a cat. Now Pod has been seen by a boy in a nightshirt. Can you name the book?
On Arrietty's first adventure outside her house with her father, she does the one thing she shouldn't do-- let herself be seen. What book is she in?

499. Konrad by Christine Nostlinger
What factory-made seven-year-old starts crying when his mother, Mrs. Bartolotti, sings a naughty song? His name is the title of this funny book.
In what book does Mrs. Bartolotti produce a report card from the Primary School of Zaire to prove her seven-year-old son is ready for fourth grade?

500. Yours Till Niagara Falls, Abby by Jane O'Connor
It was going to be a perfectly perfect summer for Abby, until her best friend Merle breaks her ankle and can't go with her to summer camp. Name that book!
In what book do Abby and Roberta team up to make summer camp and Buttercup Bunk something to remember?

501. Beanpole by Barbara Park
Ever since third grade, when she played the Maypole at the school pageant, Lillian Iris Pinkerton has had a special nickname which is the title of this book. Do you know it?
Lillian thinks one of her birthday wishes is coming true when B.B. Appleton asks her to dance; later she discovers that he was paid five dollars to dance with her! Name that book!

502. Bridge to Terabithia by Katherine Paterson
Leslie and Jess make a secret kingdom in the woods which they reach by swinging on a rope over a creek. What book is this?

Jess Aarons thinks he is the fastest runner in his school, until a new student beats him. On top of that, she's a girl--Leslie Burke! Name that book!

503. Courage Dana by Susan Beth Pfeffer
As a test of her bravery, Dana Parker spends part of the night in a graveyard, but it's on her way home that her bravery is really tested in this book called....
Songs, such as "Take Me Out To The Ball Game," help keep Dana's mind off being in a graveyard at night. Name that book!

504. Old Ramon by Jack Schaefer
This old sheepherder had taken care of the boy's grandfather's and father's sheep for many years. What book tells of the boy's traveling with him so he can learn all about sheepherding?
Sancho, the young black dog, is learning all about sheepherding from old Pedro, but tragedy strikes before he can use his learning. Name that book!

505. Caught in the Moving Mountains by Gloria Skurzynski
When their father sends Lance and Paul alone on a camping trip, he hopes the experience will make men out of them, especially Paulie. Name that book!
Although the dope smuggler threatens him with a gun, Paulie refuses to leave the wounded man alone in the wilderness in this book called....

506. Into the Dream by William Sleator
If you've ever thought it would be wonderful to have ESP, you might change your mind after reading this book where Paul and Francine develop ESP after they encounter a UFO! Name that book!
Paul and Francine are forced to become friends because of a dream. It seems that they have the same nightmare night after night. That's strange enough, but things get worse when they discover the dream is being sent to them by a dog! Name that book!

507. Help! There's a Cat Washing in Here by Allison Smith
Henry Walker's not afraid of cooking, cleaning, washing, or even Baby Ruth Carson. Henry's not afraid of anything--except cats! What book is this?
Aunt Wilhemina wants to move in and take care of the

Walker family since Henry, Joe, and Annie's mother
must get a job. Name the book in which Henry must
cook a perfect dinner to prove to his aunt that she
isn't needed.

508. Angie's First Case by Donald Sobol
    Angie and Jess escape from Charlie, a vicious guard
dog, by feeding him pieces of hamburgers. Name that
book!
    When Angie jogs, she sometimes drops the ten pen-
nies she carries in her handkerchief. If you've read
this book you know why. What is its title?

509. Call It Courage by Armstrong Sperry
    In what book does Mafatu brave a storm and the
rigors of living on a desert island to prove his courage
to his people and to himself?
    A necklace of shark's teeth helps Mafatu return a
hero to his island home. This adventure is called....

510. Always Abigail by Joyce St. Peter
    First Abigail puts a blob of finger paint on Prissy
Parker's nose, then her entire fifth-grade class starts
painting each other. When Mr. B.B. Byrd, the prin-
cipal, walks in, Abigail can't resist painting him too!
Name that book!
    Abigail doesn't want to spend her summer at Camp
Sycamore because it's a fat camp for overweight people.
What book is she in?

511. The Noonday Friends by Mary Stolz
    In what book does Franny take care of her little
brother, Marshall, every day after school, which leaves
very little time for friends?
    In which book does Franny's father get fired from
his job as a shoe salesman for telling a customer she
looks terrible?

512. The Lost Legend of Finn by Mary Tannen
    Their mother will not tell Fiona and her brother
anything about the father they have never seen, so with
the help of a Druid chant and a magic book, they go
looking for him. Name that book!
    Old Biddy Gwynn turns Fiona McCool and her brother
into ravens and sends them into the story of the red
doe and Finn. Can you name this book?

513. The Trouble with Tuck by Theodore Taylor
        Helen is convinced that her parents are going to have
      her dog, Tuck, put to sleep because he is blind. Name
      the book in which she takes Tuck and runs away from
      home to save his life.
        Helen first suspects that her dog, Friar Tuck, is
      going blind when he crashes through the family's screen
      door. What book is this?

514. The Best Bad Thing by Yoshiko Uchida
        In this book Abu, a Japanese boy, almost loses an
      arm because of a dangerous game he and his brother
      play with freight trains. What is its title?
        Rinko is sure her summer is ruined because she has
      to stay with crazy Mrs. Hata and her two young sons,
      Zenny and Abu, in this book called....

515. A Jar of Dreams by Yoshiko Uchida
        Rinko learns about the hatred some Americans feel
      toward Japanese people when her brother's dog is killed.
      Name that book!
        Rinko doesn't want to be Japanese. She hates her
      black hair and wants to be like her American classmates,
      until Aunt Waka visits from Japan. What book is she in?

516. A Dog Called Kitty by Bill Wallace
        The scars on Ricky's face, arms, and back are not
      all that remain of the dog attack he suffered as a small
      child. There is also his fear of all dogs, which makes
      his father view him as a coward. Name that book!
        In what book does Ricky's little brother, Chuckie,
      give him the idea to use hot peppers to teach his dog
      to stay away from coyote traps?

517. The Long Winter by Laura Ingalls Wilder
        Laura is almost fourteen and meets Almanzo Wilder in
      this book, entitled....
        In what book do the Ingalls have to wait until May
      to celebrate Christmas because blizzards cut off the
      trains?

518. These Happy Golden Years by Laura Ingalls Wilder
        Even in blowing snow and -40 degree weather, Al-
      manzo always comes in his sleigh to bring Laura home
      from her teaching job on the weekends. Which book is
      this?

Laura agrees to marry Almanzo, but only if the preacher does not use the word "obey" in the wedding ceremony. This book is entitled....

519. <u>C.L.U.T.Z.</u> by Marilyn Wilkes
The robot in this book is one of the first to be programmed to have all the positive emotions that humans have. He is very nice and polite; he even has a sense of humor. If only that spring didn't stick out of his ear and if only he weren't so clumsy! Name that book!
This robot tries very hard to please the Pentax family. After all, it is a robot's purpose to serve and please humans. But just between you and me, he'd better not mess up or off he goes to the recycling plant. Can you name this book?

CHAPTER V

SIXTH GRADE

EASIER READING

520. The Wolves of Willoughby Chase by Joan Aiken
In which book does Sylvia watch in horror as a
wolf jumps through a window right into her train com-
partment?
First, the evil governess, Miss Slighcarp, sent the
servants away and sold all of Bonnie's toys. Now she
is ready to get rid of Bonnie and Sylvia. Name that
book!

521. Tuck Everlasting by Natalie Babbitt
In what book is Winnie Foster kidnapped by Mae
Tuck and her two sons, Jesse and Miles, because Winnie sees Jesse drinking water from a very unusual
spring?
In this family no one gets any older than they were
a certain day eighty-six years ago. Can you name the
book in which a girl named Winnie discovers their secret?

522. The Indian in the Cupboard by Lynne Reid Banks
The Indian has black, fierce eyes; he wears buckskin leggings and a headband with a feather. In fact,
he looks exactly like a real Indian except for one thing
--he's less than three inches tall. Name that book!
A small key and a small, white metal cupboard; two
ordinary objects that used together make plastic toys
come to life, in this book called....

523. By Crumbs, It's Mine! by Patricia Beatty
In what book does Demaris' father desert his family
to search for gold, leaving them on a train headed toward Arizona Territory and unknown dangers?

When thirteen-year-old Demaris Boyd is given a
white elephant, she thinks it is a joke. But the elephant turns out to be a hotel and it's no joke. In
what book does this happen?

524. Eight Mules from Monterey by Patricia Beatty
When Mr. Murfree, in a drunken state, chops his
foot, it looks like the end of the line for Fayette, her
mother, and the Monterey library, until they meet the
Possum. What book are they in?
The ladies of Big Tree Junction are desperate for
books, so a library is carried to them on mules. Can
you name this book?

525. That's One Ornery Orphan by Patricia Beatty
Hallie Lee Baker is adopted by three different fam-
ilies and each time she messes up and is returned to the
orphanage. One time she dunks a preacher in the river,
another time she mixes up all the babies, and another
time she ruins a stage performance. What book is this?
In what book is Hallie Lee Baker afraid of being
adopted by a German farmer because she thinks he
wants to hitch her to a plow and make her plow his
fields?

526. Getting to Know Me by Elizabeth T. Billington
Peter knows that the bully of Great Barrington,
Bobby Schumacher, is just waiting to find him alone
so that he can beat him up, in this book called....
Peter always carries a camera and takes lots of pho-
tographs. Is it because he likes to take photos or is
he just trying to be like his father? Name the book.

527. It's Not the End of the World by Judy Blume
Karen Newman's parents still love her, her brother
Jeff, and her sister Amy, but they don't love each
other any more, and the three children are caught in
the middle of their fights. Can you name that book?
In her Day Book, Karen gives every day a grade,
and her days have all been "D's" since her parents
decided to get a divorce. What is the title of this
novel?

528. Then Again, Maybe I Won't by Judy Blume
When thirteen-year-old Tony Miglione's father becomes

rich from an invention, Tony finds out that having a
lot of money brings with it many problems. Name that
book!

Corky's in love with thirteen-year-old Tony, but
Tony's in love with Lisa who lives next door. The only
problem is, she is sixteen. What is the title?

529. Alone in Wolf Hollow by Dana Brookins
Uncle Charlie agrees to let newly orphaned Arnie
and Bart come live with him. In what book do the boys
arrive at Uncle Charlie's only to discover that he is an
alcoholic and doesn't remember them?

On Halloween Eve, Bart and Arnie discover a dead
body in the woods during their daily walk to school!
Name that book!

530. The Animal, the Vegetable and John D. Jones by Betsy
Byars
John D. Jones dislikes Clara and Deanie, the daughters of his mother's boyfriend, but he is worried when,
later, one of them is missing. Name that book!

Stepsisters are the last thing John D. Jones wants,
so to make a bad first impression he resolves to speak
to them only in sentences of five words. Can you name
this book?

531. The Cybil War by Betsy Byars
Love can be a terrible thing; especially in this book
where it turns two best friends, Tony and Simon, into
rivals for the affections of Cybil. Can you name it?

Simon loves Cybil Ackerman, but Tony tricks him
into taking Harriet Haywood to a movie so that Tony
can take Cybil. What book are they in?

532. The House of Wings by Betsy Byars
Sammy's grandfather's house has geese in the living-
room, a parrot in the kitchen, and an owl in the bathroom. In what book will you find his unusual house?

What began for Sammy as an effort to run away from
his grandfather, ends up in an exciting capture of a
wounded crane. Name that book!

533. The Night Swimmers by Betsy Byars
In what book does Retta find a swimming pool for her
and her brothers to swim in at night when its owner is

asleep? That is, she thinks he is asleep until a bright floodlight comes on.

As little Roy, eager to surprise his brother and sister, hurls himself off the diving board into the colonel's pool, he never once remembers that he can't swim. What book is this?

534. The Summer of the Swans by Betsy Byars
In what book does Sara's little brother, Charlie, who is retarded, get lost while looking for some beautiful birds?

Sara forgets about her horrible hair, her flat face and her big feet when her retarded little brother, Charlie, disappears in the night. Name that book!

535. Pinch by Larry Callen
What boy wants to buy a pig so he can train it to hunt? His name is the name of the book.

Training a pig is just like training a dog, according to Mr. Grimball. And sure enough, Homer the pig soon learns to hunt as well as any hound. Name that book!

536. Fireball by John Christopher
When Brad and Simon step toward the large ball of glowing light it transports them to a parallel world in this book called....

Cousins Brad and Simon hate each other until they find themselves transported to a parallel world where they must help each other survive. Can you name this book?

537. Deadly Game at Stony Creek by Peter Zachary Cohen
The gray dog and his pack terrorize the countryside, and one of their attacks leaves Karla Dodley crippled for life. When danger threatens, the dogs escape into the woods, but this time two frightened high-school boys are in their way! Name that book!

In this book a gray dog grows too large and too fierce, so his owners dump him in the country. Four hard years later he is the leader of a pack of five wild dogs. Hunger makes anything that moves their prey-- mice, sheep, even people. What is the title of this book?

538. Lenny Kandell, Smart Aleck by Ellen Conford

Lenny is in big trouble; he's just stabbed Aunt Harriet's fur piece with his new pocketknife! Name that book!

When Lenny tripped the boy in the movie theatre, he didn't know it was Mousie Blatner, THE Mousie Blatner who kills people. Name that book!

539. The Luck of Pokey Bloom by Ellen Conford
Name the book in which Charlotte Bloom is convinced that she can win a $10,000 contest prize simply by thinking about the prize three times a day.

This book tells about a girl who loves entering contests, and her big brother, Gordon, who uses the closet for a phone booth and likes health food and yoga. Can you name it?

540. Come to the Edge by Julia Cunningham
In what book is ten-year-old Gravel Winter left at a foster home by his father who thinks Gravel is "a stone around my neck"?

In this book, Gravel Winter saves Mr. Gant's life, an act that later involves him in a murder. Can you give the title?

541. The Cat Ate My Gymsuit by Paula Danziger
Marcy hated school and herself until Ms. Finney came along, but now Ms. Finney is about to be fired. Name that book!

When Marcy Lewis' favorite teacher is suspended, Marcy forgets about being shy and becomes a fighter. Can you name this book?

542. The Pistachio Prescription by Paula Danziger
Cassandra Stephens thinks she is an ugly duckling, but she finally gets a boyfriend, wins a school election and feels good about herself. Then her parents announce that they're getting a divorce. What book is she in?

When her parents fight, Cassandra usually gets severe asthma attacks that can only be brought under control with medicine. Name the book in which Cassandra wishes for a prescription to cure all their family problems.

543. There's a Bat in Bunk Five by Paula Danziger
Ginger Simon is the biggest troublemaker of all the

campers at Camp Serendipity, where Marcy is a counselor-in-training. Can you name the book in which Ginger is assigned to Marcy's cabin?
Name the book in which Marcy's pantyhose start to fall down while she is on her first date with Ted. Clue: Both of them are counselors at Camp Serendipity.

544. Gone-Away Lake by Elizabeth Enright
Lost in a mosquito-infested swamp, Julian and Portia discover not only a mysterious Latin inscription on a rock but also a ghost town! Name that book!
In what book does Portia's little brother, Foster, wander into the Gulper, a bog of quicksand in the swamp?

545. Go to the Room of the Eyes by Betty K. Erwin
When Susan pulls down the window shade, a mysterious note falls out which starts the Evans children on a strange treasure hunt begun thirty years earlier. What is the title of this book?
In what book do Jody and Susan go looking for a pot of gold at the end of a rainbow and find stolen candlesticks from the cathedral instead?

546. The Great Brain by John D. Fitzgerald
Name the book which tells about the first water closet (indoor toilet) in Adenville, Utah, and how Tom made a fortune from it in three days.
The whole town is cheering Tom D. for rescuing the Jensen boys from Skeleton Cave, but J.D. thinks his dog, Brownie, deserves some credit too. Name that book!

547. Harriet the Spy by Louise Fitzhugh
Harriet M. Welsch is only in sixth grade, but she is preparing to be a great writer--by taking notes on everyone she sees. Name that book!
Janie, who has her own chemistry set and is planning to blow up the world some day; Sport, who cooks, cleans, and manages his father's money; and Harriet, who has fourteen notebooks full of notes on people, are all friends in a funny book called....

548. Graven Images by Paul Fleischman
When the Orion docked at New Bethany, the entire

crew, except for the binnacle boy, were found to be
dead. Name that book!
Name the book in which Zorelli the sculptor is hired
to carve a statue of a ghost!

549. Humbug Mountain by Sid Fleischman
In what book is Wiley captured by the dirtiest, meanest outlaws of the Old West, Shagnasty and the Fool
Killer?
In this Wild West adventure, a ghost teaches crows
to talk, eats chicken and biscuits, and even saves the
whole Flint family from two desperados. Can you name
the book?

550. The Stone-Faced Boy by Paula Fox
In the first grade Gus discovered that if he erased
all expression from his face, the other children would
leave him alone. But now it has become impossible to
smile or cry. Name his story.
Animals love his little sister, Serena, so why do they
always growl, bark, or hiss at Gus? What is the title
of his story?

551. Blue Willow by Doris Gates
Janey had no brothers or sisters and not many things
to be proud of. The only beautiful thing she owned
was a plate, which she kept carefully packed in her
suitcase. What is the title of this book?
More than anything else, Janey wanted to stay in one
place long enough to have friends and go to school.
But to migrant farm workers, it seemed an impossible
dream. Name her story.

552. How I Put My Mother Through College by Corrine Gerson
When Jessica's mom starts college, she turns to Jessica for advice on everything. In fact, Jessica starts
to think she's become her mother's mother in this book
called....
When Jessica's mother becomes a college cheerleader,
she breaks her arm and is carried home by a football
player. Name that book!

553. Do Bananas Chew Gum? by Jamie Gilson
While Sam Mott is at the orthodontist's, a tornado
strikes the neighborhood where he is supposed to be

babysitting. In what book does he find his young
charges in good health but terrified because they think
they caused the storm by touching their father's stereo?
   In what book do Sam Mott, Alicia Bliss, and Wally
dig through the school cafeteria's garbage trying to
find Wally's retainer?

554. Savage Sam by Fred Gipson
   After a fierce battle with a wildcat, Arliss and Travis turn around to face a greater danger--Indians!
What book is this?
   In what book does Arliss Coates bite an Apache's
ear completely off while standing on his shoulders and
pulling his hair?

555. Who Will Take Care of Me? by Patricia Hermes
   Name the book in which Mark's brother Peter gets
lost in the woods by their lake cottage, and Mark pan-
ics because Peter is mentally handicapped.
   After their grandmother dies, Mark takes his brother
Peter and runs away because he doesn't want Peter taken
away to a special school. Can you name the book?

556. Circle of Fire by William H. Hooks
   Picking walnuts for his Grandma's Christmas fruit-
cakes turns out to be quite an adventure for Harrison
and his two black friends, Kitty and Scrap Fisher. On
the way home Bud Highsmith holds them at gun point
and demands that they give him the walnuts. Name
that book!
   When Harrison Hawkins fights the Gypsy boy Liam,
he pulls Liam's hair and reveals an ugly cut in the shape
of a cross on the top of Liam's head. What book is
this?

557. Hang On, Harvey! by Nancy J. Hopper
   Name the book in which Harvey spends a lot of time
developing a crazy look to scare off a bully named Jon
Jamison.
   In this book, eighth grade isn't going very well for
Harvey Smucker. He doesn't get to be principal flutist,
his best friend falls for his girl, and Jon Jamison starts
to bully him. What is the title?

558. The Gammage Cup by Carol Kendall
   There are only four Minnipins who know their land

is in danger of attack from beyond the Sunset Mountains,
and no one will believe them. What book are they in?
   Name the book in which Mingy is caught by the Mushroom people, who are coming to invade the Minnipins'
land.

559. The Forgotten Door by Alexander Key
   Name the book in which the Bean family meets a boy
who has clothes that won't tear, has never seen cars or
money, and can communicate with animals.
   Little Jon fell through a hole in the blackness and
landed on a strange planet he does not understand,
where people lie and lock their doors against thieves
and make war. Name his story.

560. Mom, the Wolf Man and Me by Norma Klein
   Brett likes living alone with her mother. They get
along very nicely until the Wolf Man comes along. What
book is this?
   Neither Evelyn nor Brett have fathers who live at
home. Evelyn desperately wants a father while Brett
definitely doesn't, especially when she meets the Wolf
Man. What book are they in?

561. The Last Battle by C.S. Lewis
   In what book does Shift the ape make Puzzle the
donkey wear a lion skin so the beasts will think that
Aslan has returned?
   In this book Farsight the eagle tells King Tirian that
the evil Calormenes have conquered Cair Paravel and
that Narnia is no more. What is the title?

562. The Lion, the Witch and the Wardrobe by C.S. Lewis
   Four children--Peter, Susan, Edmund and Lucy--
find a wardrobe that leads to the mysterious land of
Narnia. What is the book's title?
   A faun named Mr. Tumnus has orders from the White
Witch to catch humans and turn them over to her. What
book is this?

563. Ronia, the Robber's Daughter by Astrid Lindgren
   Only Hell's Gap separates two rival gangs of robbers
and their children, Birk and Ronia, in this book called....
   Name the book in which Birk and Ronia take turns
jumping over Hell's Gap until one of them falls in.

564. Anastasia at Your Service by Lois Lowry
     Anastasia seeks a job as companion to a rich old lady,
     but Mrs. Bellingham hires her as a maid! Name that
     book!
     In what book does Anastasia wear her mother's bra,
     stuffed with pantyhose, to Daphne's birthday party?

565. A Summer to Die by Lois Lowry
     When Molly comes home from the hospital, Meg can't
     understand why her parents put up with Molly's misbe-
     havior until they finally tell her the truth about Molly's
     sickness. Name that book!
     Thirteen-year-old Meg always feels that her pretty
     sister, Molly, has everything going for her, until she
     is told that Molly is dying. What is the title?

566. Arthur for the Very First Time by Patricia MacLachlan
     Name the book in which Arthur's Uncle Wrisby speaks
     French to his chickens and sings to his pigs.
     In this book Moria and Arthur drink a bottle of what
     they think is medicine but it turns out to be whiskey
     and causes them to throw up on Moria's grandfather's
     shoes. Can you name it?

567. The Money Room by Eloise Jarvis McGraw
     Scotty knows his great-grandfather had a hidden
     treasure somewhere on his old farm. The problem is to
     find it before someone else does. Name that book!
     Why is Dorrie Suggs so eager to buy the old farm
     from Scotty's mother? Scotty suspects it has to do with
     rumors of a hidden treasure. In what book does a para-
     keet help solve the mystery?

568. The Turquoise Toad Mystery by Georgess McHargue
     When Ben agreed to spend his summer vacation in
     the middle of an Arizona desert as part of an archaeo-
     logical dig, he didn't count on becoming involved with
     thieves. Name that book!
     Ben's love for Frito, his pet Coatimundi, increases
     when Frito eats a poisonous bark scorpion placed in
     Ben's boot by someone who wants him out of the way.
     Can you name that book?

569. Save Queen of Sheba by Louise Moeri
     In what book does twelve-year-old King David have

to face an Indian woman who is holding a knife to his
little sister's throat?
    Can you name the book in which a twelve-year-old
boy and his little sister set off on foot to find Oregon
and their parents after an Indian attack on their wagon
train?

570. Year of the Black Pony by Walt Morey
    When the Grayson brothers begin to beat up on Mr.
Chase, Christopher jumps on Arlo Grayson's back and
sinks his teeth into Arlo's ear. What book is this?
    Because Christopher rode Lucifer in a blizzard to
bring back a teddy bear for his sick sister, Ellie, the
horse lies close to death with frosted lung. What is the
title of this book?

571. Sandy and the Rock Star by Walter Morey
    In what book will you meet Mr. McKinzie, who owns
an island and uses it as a hunting ground for imported
big-game animals?
    Paul Winters and the big cougar are trapped on Mr.
McKinzie's island. One of them is there to be killed
and one of them isn't supposed to be there at all. Name
that book!

572. Ace Hits the Big Time by B.B. Murphy
    Name the book in which Horace Hobart is unable to
face the students at his new school as his usual dull
self, so he wears an eye patch and a red jacket with a
dragon on the back.
    Horace Hobart is a funny-looking kid. At his new
school a gang called the Falcons likes to beat up the
funny-looking kids. In what book does Horace not want
to go to school?

573. Mr. Radagast Makes an Unexpected Journey by Sharon
Nastick
    Mr. Radagast, the most unpopular teacher at Mayfair
Junior High, tries to get his class to prove the theory
of immaterialism--that is, making something disappear
by thinking it out of existence. He wants them to make
a science book disappear; they want to make him disappear. What book is this?
    Did you ever wish you could make a teacher disap-
pear? That's what happens to Mr. Radagast, a teacher
in this book called....

574. The Solomon System by Phyllis Naylor
      Freeze! At Ted's summer camp, that means the first
      person who moves has to clear the tables. In this book
      Ted doesn't move even though someone sticks french
      fries up his nose. What is its title?
      Ted and Nory hate their grandmother's present,
      button-down-the-front sweaters, so much that they
      hide them in the ceiling rafters at their summer camp.
      Name that book.

575. Edgar Allan by John Neufeld
      What book tells of the Fickett family's adopting a
      little brother for their four children?
      E.A. is little and smart and the cutest baby around.
      So how can Mary Nell ignore him? Name that book!

576. It's Like This, Cat by Emily Neville
      Dave knows Crazy Kate the Cat Woman is not really
      crazy. In fact, she may be his best friend. What is
      this book's title?
      When the Mitchells get stuck in a traffic jam, Cat
      decides to jump out the car window and Dave has no
      choice but to chase him through the heavy New York
      traffic. Name that book!

577. The Black Pearl by Scott O'Dell
      Ramon Salazar thinks his dream has come true when
      he finds the great Pearl of Heaven. But then the dream
      turns into a nightmare. What is the title of this book?
      Is the magnificent pearl worth the danger? In what
      book does sixteen-year-old Ramon risk his life, first to
      get the pearl, and then to return it?

578. The Great Gilly Hopkins by Katherine Paterson
      At her third foster home in less than three years,
      Galadriel's companions are fat Maime Trotter, slow-
      learning William Ernest, and blind Mr. Randolph. Name
      her story.
      Being nice to William Ernest is just part of Gilly's
      plan to steal enough money to join her mother in San
      Francisco. What is the title of this book?

579. Yobgorgle: Mystery Monster of Lake Ontario by Daniel
      Manus Pinkwater
      Name the book in which Professor McFwain is offered

a great deal on a Hindustan-Eight motor vehicle. He
can buy it for only $3.00, as long as he agrees to wear
a chicken costume whenever he drives it.
   In what book do Professor McFwain, Colonel Ken
Krenwinkle, and Eugene Winkleman team up to go monster hunting?

580. The Strange but Wonderful Cosmic Awareness of Duffy
      Moon by Jean Robinson
         Sixth-grader Duffy is so small that a third grader
      gives him a shiner. Name the book in which he decides
      the cure for all his problems is Dr. Louis Flamel's "Home
      Study Course in Cosmic Awareness."
         Duffy thinks that Dr. Flamel's course on cosmic
      awareness has solved all his problems, then he meets
      Boots McAfee. Name that book!

581. Freaky Friday by Mary Rodgers
         In what book does thirteen-year-old Annabel Andrews
      wake up to discover that she has actually turned into
      her mother--straight teeth, curlers in the hair, and all?
         When Annabel becomes her mother for the day, she
      fires the cleaning lady, washes her father's shirts with
      the rugs, and finds herself faced with important company
      for dinner. What is the title?

582. Summer Switch by Mary Rodgers
         When Ben Andrews returns to school and has to write
      the usual "What I did over summer vacation" paper, he
      won't have any problems. He can tell what it's like to
      switch bodies with his father because that's exactly
      what he does in this book called....
         Ben switches bodies with his father. He has to go to
      to L.A. on a business trip in his father's body. His
      father, in Ben's body, has to go to Camp Soonawissaki.
      Name that book!

583. Fourteen by Marilyn Sachs
         Rebecca Cooper is embarrassed because her mother
      writes children's books--fourteen so far--about Rebecca's
      life. Name that book!
         In Rebecca's teen romances girls fall in love with
      tall, dark, good-looking boys, but she falls in love
      with a short, skinny, blond boy who cries a lot in this
      book called....

584. Weird Henry Berg by Sarah Sargent
    In what book do you find a mysterious egg, a boy
    named Henry, an old lady, and a dragon named Vincent?
    A mysterious egg hatches after being in Henry's
    family for ninety-five years. In what book does a
    dragon search for whatever hatched from the egg?

585. The Dulcimer Boy by Tor Seidler
    In which book will you find: the twins William and
    Jules, the stingy Mr. and Mrs. Carbuncle who lock the
    twins in their attic, and a sailor who was hanged but
    didn't die?
    William steals the dulcimer to keep the Carbuncles
    from selling it. When they catch him he runs away,
    leaving his twin, Jules, at the mercy of the stingy
    couple. Name that book!

586. The White Stag by Kate Seredy
    In what book is a small boy blinded when he sees
    visions of the future in the form of eagles and white
    herons?
    What book tells of Attila the Conqueror, who slew
    thousands with his sword as he led his people to their
    promised land?

587. Lost in the Devil's Desert by Gloria Skurzynski
    Kevin is relieved to get away from two escaped con-
    victs, but then he realizes he has been abandoned in
    the desert, far away from the highway. Can you name
    this book?
    Kevin likes T-shirts with funny slogans, so when he
    sees the two men wearing Mountain State Penitentiary
    T-shirts, he doesn't think they might really be escaped
    convicts until he sees them rob old Barney's store.
    What book is he in?

588. The First Hard Times by Doris Buchanan Smith
    Ancil's friend Lloyd has had two stepfathers, almost
    three. Ancil only has one, Harvey, whom she hates,
    in this book called....
    Ancil's dislike for her stepfather, Harvey, increases
    when he tosses her in the sea. Because she can't swim,
    she almost drowns. Name that book!

589. The Egypt Game by Zilpha K. Snyder

Name the book in which Melanie hides her friend
April's false eyelashes so she won't wear them to school.
When a child is murdered in the neighborhood, the
people on Orchard Avenue begin to suspect the Professor. But April, Melanie, and Elizabeth believe he is
innocent. What book are they in?

590. The Headless Cupid by Zilpha K. Snyder
David's new stepsister, Amanda, offers to teach him
and his little brother and sisters about the occult, but
only if they go through nine ordeals. Name that book!
Amanda, who is never excited about anything, sud-
denly becomes enthusiastic when she finds out that the
old Westerly house where they live once had a polter-
geist. What is the title?

591. The Witches of Worm by Zilpha K. Snyder
Is Jessica's cat really a cat, or is it a devil, making
her do evil things? This book is called....
In what book does twelve-year-old Jessica perform an
exorcism ceremony on her cat?

592. Miracles on Maple Hill by Virginia Sorenson
When Marly decides to surprise the family with pan-
cakes on the old wood-burning stove, she forgets to
open the damper and fills the house with smoke, in this
book called....
In what book does the truant officer, Annie-get-
your-gun, arrange for the school children to help with
the maple sugaring when Mr. Chris falls sick?

593. Peppermints in the Parlor by Barbara Brooks Wallace
The smell of peppermints tells Emily that Tilly must
be the spy who told cruel Mrs. Meeching about Emily's
hidden coins and how she tried to help the old people.
And now Tilly is going to drown Emily's kitten! Name
that book!
When Emily returns to Sugar Hill Hall, she discovers
it has been turned into a frightening and dangerous old
people's home. Which book is this?

594. Toby Lived Here by Hilma Wolitzer
Toby's mother is crazy sick and there's no hope for
a cure. In this book, Toby hopes that she and her
little sister, Anne, can stay together, but no relative
wants both girls. Can you name it?

Toby is ashamed because her mother is in a mental hospital and she has to live with foster parents, so she lies about her home life to her new, rich friend, Susan, in this book called....

595. Happily Ever After--Almost by Judie Wolkoff
During a football game, Sarah Birdsall dries her wet hair with her underwear and a hot-air hand dryer in a public restroom. Name that book!
RJ is a very rich eleven year old. Name the book in which he would give up all his riches if he could get away from his mean mother and live with his father and new stepsisters, Kitty and Sarah.

596. The Secret Window by Betty Ren Wright
In this book Meg knows her brother Bill will win the science contest because she dreams that he does, and her dreams often foretell the future. The title is....
Name the book in which Meg is accused of vandalism at the art museum because she is dressed exactly like Gracie, her best friend.

ADVANCED READING

597. The Magic of the Glits by Carole S. Adler
Not only does Jeremy have to put up with a cast on his leg, but now his mother saddles him with a seven-year-old girl to entertain for the summer. Name his story.
In what book does Jeremy try to teach Lynette how to cook breakfast for Dave, in hopes that Dave will then find her useful and not send her to an orphanage?

598. Is There Life on a Plastic Planet? by Mildred Ames
Hollis has been replaced at school and home by a life-size doll that is her exact duplicate. Hollis wants the doll to disappear but it won't until she can find something she does better than the doll. Can you name this book?
The life-size doll is an exact duplicate of Hollis, down to the tiniest detail, except that it does everything perfectly, unlike poor, overweight Hollis. What book is she in?

599. In the Circle of Time by Margaret J. Anderson
     Jennifer and Robert want to help Kartan's people,
     but first they must find a way to escape the Barbaric
     Ones. Name that book!
     Robert, from Scotland, and an American girl, Jenni-
     fer, discover a mysterious circle made by thirteen an-
     cient stones with magical powers which can transport
     people through time. Can you name this book?

600. Tina Gogo by Judie Angell
     She lies, she steals, she hits little boys in the face.
     Her name is Bettina Gogolavsky but don't call her that.
     Call her by her nick-name which is also the name of this
     book. What is it?
     Sarajane Punch was afraid of Bettina Gogolavsky
     from the first time she saw her. She wants nothing to
     do with the girl but Bettina won't leave her alone. In
     fact, Bettina even starts to work at the Punch family
     restaurant. This book is called....

601. Sounder by William Armstrong
     This book, set in the Depression years, tells of a
     black man who is chained and thrown into jail for steal-
     ing a ham to feed his hungry family. What is the title?
     In what book is a faithful coon hound shot by a
     deputy who is hauling his master to jail in the back of
     a truck?

602. Just Like Jenny by Sandy Asher
     Name the book in which Stephanie Nordland is jealous
     of her best friend, Jenny Gianino, because she thinks
     Jenny is the better dancer of the two.
     Stephanie Nordland seems to have the talent and ded-
     ication to achieve her dream of becoming a professional
     dancer--until something scares her. What book is she
     in?

603. Shelter from the Wind by Marion Dane Bauer
     The hardest thing Stacy has ever had to do in her
     whole life is drown the puppy. It happens in the book
     called....
     In what book does Stacy drink a bottle of whiskey
     because she wants to see if she is like her mother?

604. Carrie's War by Nina Bawden
     In what book are Carrie and Nick sent away from

London during World War II to live with mean old Mr.
Evans who has loose false teeth?

What book set in England during World War II has
these characters: Carrie and Nick Willow, Hepzibah
Green, Mister Johnny Gotobed, and Albert Sandwich?

605. The Robbers by Nina Bawden
      Philip was too young and his grandmother too old
to win a fight with his father. Name the book in which
Philip must leave his castle home to live with his father
and stepmother in London.

      Philip knows stealing is wrong, but not stealing
would mean being a traitor to Darcy, his best friend,
so he climbs through the window into the attic next
door. Name that book!

606. Squib by Nina Bawden
      In what book does a strange little boy with one
brown eye and one blue eye mysteriously remind Kate
of her drowned brother?

      Is Kate seeing ghosts? Robin thinks so, until he
sees the little boy's face high in the window at the
Old People's Home. Name that book!

607. Jonathan Down Under by Patricia Beatty
      It's 1851 and the California gold rush has not been
successful for Jonathan Cole and his father. The Aus-
tralian gold rush has just begun and much against Jonathan's wishes, that is where they're bound. Name
that book.

      Thirteen-year-old Jonathan Cole has many adventures
while mining for gold in Australia with his father, Charlie. They include blindness, murder, being left to die
in the wilderness, and camping next to convicts, one of
whom always wears a sack over his head. Can you name
this book?

608. The Curse of the Blue Figurine by John Bellairs
      Johnny wishes on the mummy figurine that Eddie
Tompke, a bully, will break his neck. The next day
Eddie's arm is broken in this book called....

      Name the book in which a strange little man with
hypnotic eyes talks Johnny into praying every day over
a mummy figurine and makes him wear an enchanted
ring.

609. The Figure in the Shadows by John Bellairs
      An old coin found in his great-grandfather's trunk
      turns out to have powerful magic, but Lewis doesn't
      want Rosa Rita to know. Name that book!
      Name the book in which Uncle Jonathon tells how
      Grandpa Barnavelt's life was saved by a poker game.

610. The House with a Clock in Its Walls by John Bellairs
      The mysterious figure pounding on the walls in the
      dead of night turns out to be Uncle Jonathon! On his
      first night in his new home, Lewis wonders if his uncle
      is crazy. What book are they in?
      In what book does Lewis have to find a clock that
      the evil sorcerer Isaac Izard has hidden? The clock
      ticks off the minutes for the end of the world.

611. The Mummy, the Will, and the Crypt by John Bellairs
      A chess set, a Greek newspaper, and a sign from a
      tea shop are clues to where Mr. H. Bagwell Glomus has
      hidden his will, the will Johnny Dixon is determined to
      find in this book called....
      In what book does Johnny Dixon battle the Guardian,
      a creature summoned by Black Magic, which turns hu-
      mans into brown, withered husks with holes for eyes?

612. A Gathering of Days: A New England Girl's Journal,
      1830-32 by Joan W. Blos
      This book is thirteen-year-old Catherine Hall's diary
      which tells of New England life in the early 1800's.
      What is the title?
      When the Shipmans' pies are stolen, Asa takes the
      blame in order to protect a runaway whom he has never
      even seen. Name that book!

613. Caddie Woodlawn by Carol Ryrie Brink
      Cousin Annabelle from Boston does very well at turn-
      ing somersaults in the hay until Caddie slips an egg down
      the back of her blouse. Name that book!
      Who was the red-headed tomboy who had many ex-
      citing and funny adventures growing up in the woods
      of western Wisconsin in the 1800's? Her name is the
      title of the book.

614. The Secret Garden by Frances H. Burnett
      In what book does nine-year-old Mary Lennox wake

up to discover that a cholera epidemic has left her completely alone and forgotten in her home in India?
Two things about Misselthwaite Manor puzzle Mary--a garden that has been locked for ten years and the mysterious crying from somewhere in the huge old house. Name that book!

615. The Pinballs by Betsy Byars
Harvey has two broken legs because of his father; Thomas J. doesn't know whom he belongs to, and Carlie was knocked unconscious by her stepfather. In what book do these three get together in a foster home?
Mrs. Mason thought tough-talking Carlie could help Harvey, who had been run over by his own father. But Carlie has problems of her own. Name that book!

616. Empty World by John Christopher
In what book does Neil Miller think he is the only survivor of a plague that causes people to die of old age in less than a week, even babies?
When Neil Miller's family is killed in a car wreck, he's sure nothing worse can happen to him, then the plague comes and everyone begins to die of old age. Name that book!

617. The White Mountains by John Christopher
In what book will you meet Will Parker who will be capped by the Tripods on his fourteenth birthday?
Will Parker thinks there is no hope that he can escape the horrible fate that awaits all Earthlings when they reach their 14th birthday. Then he meets a man called Ozymandias. Name that book!

618. Seven Daughters and Seven Sons by Barbara Cohen and Bahija Lovejoy
Name the book in which a father gives his daughter the white ivory queen from his chess set to keep as a talisman until she returns from a long journey.
In what book does Buran, a girl from Baghdad, have to disguise herself as a man so that she can earn money for her parents and six sisters?

619. Anything for a Friend by Ellen Conford
In what book do Wallis and Stuffy type love letters to a girl they call Ruth the Doof and sign them with their teacher's name?

Can you name the book in which Wallis has to move
into a house where a murder has taken place? Clue:
She holds a seance in the house for her sixth-grade
classmates.

620. A Dance to Still Music by Barbara Corcoran
Margaret can't stand the thought of going to a special school for the deaf, something she will have to do
when her mother marries Ed, so she runs away. This
book is called....
When runaway Margaret stops to help the wounded
fawn, she has no idea that they will both find a home
on a boat with a woman named Josie. Name that book!

621. The Person in the Potting Shed by Barbara Corcoran
A strange and timid woman in the woods, a nocturnal
visitor who slashes a portrait, and a dead body that
disappears--in what book will you find these and other
mysteries at an old plantation where Franklin and Dorothy
are spending their summer?
When Franklin and Dorothy found Old Francois lying
on the floor, they thought he was drunk again and had
passed out. They didn't know that he had been murdered. Can you name that book?

622. The Silent Voice by Julia Cunningham
In what book is Phillipe so jealous of Auguste's talent as a dancer that he threatens to cripple him so that
Auguste can't walk, let alone dance?
Can you name the book in which Auguste's most
precious possession is a gold medallion from his mime
teacher?

623. Ghost Lane by Jane Louise Curry
In what book is eleven-year-old Richard Morgan invited to tea by Mr. Drew, the Morgan's landlord, so he
can see a ghost?
When Goslings House is burglarized, the papers say
it was the Ghost Mob, while others believe there are
real ghosts in the old manor. Either way, Richard, who
is a Junior Detective, is determined to get to the bottom of it. Name that mystery!

624. Conrad's War by Andrew Davies
Name the book in which Conrad and his father discover

a time leak and have an identical dream that takes them
smack into the middle of World War II.
   Conrad is not keen on his dad, the great writer,
but he is keen on these things: violence, wars, the
army, killing, guns, and Towzer, his dog. In fact he
is so keen on wars that he decides to build his own
tank. What book is he in?

625. The Door in the Wall by Marguerite De Angeli
      This story, set in the middle ages, tells of Robin
      who plans to become a knight until an illness leaves
      him crippled. Can you name it?
      In what book does a crippled boy set out to save
      Sir Peter's castle from attacking Welshmen?

626. The House of Sixty Fathers by Meindert DeJong
      Saving only the family pig, three ducklings, and a
      little stone mill, Tien Pao's family races toward an empty
      sampan as the Japanese invaders set fire to their village.
      So begins the book named....
      What book tells the exciting story of Tien Pao, a
      small Chinese boy, who, lost, starving, and terrified
      of being found by Japanese soldiers, sets out to find
      his family?

627. The Wheel on the School by Meindert DeJong
      Will just wondering make things begin to happen?
      The six school children in Shora, Holland, find out
      when they wonder about storks in a book called....
      In what book are Pier and Dirk, the twins, chased
      by a legless man in a wheelchair?

628. The Twenty-One Balloons by William Pene Du Bois
      What book tells of the astounding adventures of Pro-
      fessor William Waterman Sherman, who starts out in a
      balloon to cross the Pacific and ends up floating in the
      Atlantic with twenty deflated balloons?
      When Professor Sherman in his balloon house wants
      to rise above the rain clouds, he simply dumps out his
      garbage. Name that book!

629. The Absolutely Perfect Horse by Marylois Dunn
      Dogmeat, that's all the old horse is good for after
      thirty-five years, but Annie saves him from the dog-
      meat men in this book called....

Petey can't believe Annie. She's always wanted a horse and now, when she finally has enough money, she buys a broken-down thirty-five-year-old nag that's fit only for dogmeat. Name that book!

630. Tales From Silver Lands by Charles J. Finger
This is a collection of folktales from the Indians of South America. One tells of how the rat had a tail like a horse. Can you give the title of the book?
One of the stories in this collection tells of an Indian tribe's turning themselves into gentle huanacos so they can escape the fierce yellow men. What is the book's title?

631. How Many Miles to Babylon? by Paula Fox
Name the book in which Gino, Stick, and Blue make James help them steal dogs so they can collect the rewards offered for their return.
In what book is James Douglas locked in a funhouse in Coney Island with Gino, Tick, and Blue--and three stolen dogs?

632. Homesick: My Own Story by Jean Fritz
Jean is born in China but she longs to see America, the home of her parents, in this book called....
In what book does Jean befriend a little Chinese boy and teach him to call her "American friend" instead of "foreign devil"?

633. My Side of the Mountain by Jean Craighead George
What book would you be in if you knew a raccoon named Jessie Coon James, a weasel named The Baron, and a falcon named Frightful?
In what book does a boy run away from home and live on his own in a hollow tree?

634. Old Yeller by Fred Gipson
The big stray dog was good for nothing but stealing meat and swimming in the spring water. In what book is Travis determined to get rid of him?
The bear cub's mother is crashing toward five-year-old Arliss with murder in her eye, and Travis is too far away to help. His only hope is his pet dog. Name that book!

635. The Iceberg and Its Shadow by Jan Greenberg
     Name the book in which Rachel breaks the unwritten
     law of her sixth-grade class when she tells the teacher
     that Mindy copied her math worksheets.
     In this book the Fabulous Foursome becomes the
     Three Musketeers when Mindy Gottfried gets mad at
     Anabeth Blair and forces her out of the group. What
     is its title?

636. Get On Out of Here, Philip Hall by Bette Greene
     Beth Lambert is already standing up to receive the
     Abner Jerome Brady Leadership Award and a $300
     scholarship when the winner is announced ... and it
     isn't her! Name that book!
     In what book do Beth Lambert and the Pretty Pen-
     nies bring excitement to Pocahontas, Arkansas, with
     a parade and a relay race between the girls and the
     boys?

637. Beat the Turtle Drum by Constance C. Greene
     Joss' dream is to own a horse, but she can only af-
     ford to rent one for a week and keep it in the garage.
     Can you name this book?
     As payment to her father for letting her rented horse
     take the car's place in the garage, Joss promises him
     the first ride. What book is this?

638. Will the Real Gertrude Hollings Please Stand Up? by
     Sheila Greenwald
     In what book does Gertrude try something called
     "sibling preparation" on her cousin Albert, who will
     soon get a little brother or sister?
     Name the book in which Gertrude convinces her
     cousin Albert that there is a thunderbolt in the bath-
     tub and that he must never go near the tub.

639. Danza by Lynn Hall
     He can't eat, his hair falls out, his hooves fall off,
     and he can no longer stand upright, but the beautiful
     Paso Fino stallion refuses to die. What book is he in?
     In what book does drinking cold water from an ice
     chest almost destroy Paulo Camacho's beautiful stallion?

640. Speaking of Snapdragons by Sheila Hayes
     One Halloween, years ago, Thomas Worthington Duffy

scared some children so badly that everyone has left
the old man alone since that night. Then one day he
speaks to Heather Mallory, the main character in this
book. Can you name it?

Heather Mallory and Marshall Benedict have been
best friends since kindergarten. They have a lot in
common, including not having fathers. Then Marshall's
mother remarries and Marshall acquires a new father,
whom Heather hates. Can you name this book?

641. Dinah and the Green Fat Kingdom by Isabelle Holland
What book tells about Dinah Randall, who is at least
thirty-two pounds overweight and keeps a stash of
cookies and candy bars in the bottom of her dirty-
clothes bag?

If Dinah stays off sweets for three months and visits
a nutritionist, she can keep her puppy, Francis. Name
her story.

642. Sizzle and Splat by Ronald Kidd
Name the book where you will find these things: A
girl and a boy with funny nicknames who play in a
youth orchestra and the Kleiman Trumpet Concerto.
The concerto contains a puzzle; if you solve it you
win a million dollars.

Prudence plays trumpet and Arthur plays tuba in
the Pirelli Youth Orchestra. In this book they witness
a kidnapping and two attempts are made on their lives,
all because of a piece of music. Can you name the title?

643. Lassie Come-Home by Eric Knight
The collie has escaped so many times that the Duke
decides to take her to live in Scotland. In what book
does Sam Carraclough tell his son, Joe, that he'll never
see the dog again?

Instead of closing the gate, the Duke's granddaughter
opens it wide, and the faithful collie escapes once more,
but this time hundreds of miles from home. Name that
book!

644. From the Mixed-Up Files of Mrs. Basil E. Frankweiler
by E.L. Konigsburg
In this book two children run away from home to the
New York Metropolitan Museum of Art--the greatest place
in the world to hide out. Name that book!

As if running away from home were not enough,
Claudia and Jamie also become involved in the mystery
of the angel statue. What is the title?

645. The Witching Hour by Stephen Krensky
     If you were a member of the Wynd family, you
could change food that you didn't like, such as lima
beans, into food that you do like, such as ice cream.
What book would you be in?
     Peter is surprised when the hook he is wearing as
part of his pirate's costume for Halloween becomes real.
Can you name this book in which Peter's plight is part
of a plot to have all children's costumes become real?

646. Onion John by Joseph Krumgold
     This friendly old man wanders through garbage dumps
to find what he needs. His name is the name of the
book. It is....
     This old man speaks a strange language but Andy
comes to understand him. The trouble starts when
Andy's father decides the town should build him a new
home. This book is called....

647. There Are Two Kinds of Terrible by Peggy Mann
     Robbie Farley thought the worst thing in the world
had happened when he broke his arm the first day of
summer vacation, but he was wrong. His story is entitled....
     Robbie didn't mind not being close to his father,
since he and his mother got along so well. But now
his mother has died of cancer. Name this book.

648. The Island Keeper by Harry Mazer
     As an overweight rich girl, Cleo Murphy never
dreamed she would eat fish heads and kill a deer with
a handmade spear, but in this book she has to, just
to stay alive. Can you name it?
     As winter approaches, Cleo's handmade raft is her
only chance to escape Duck Island where she has lived
in solitude for the last seven months. What book is she
in?

649. Mrs. Fish, Ape and Me, the Dump Queen by Norma Fox
     Mazer
     At school, Joyce Adams has no friends because the

other kids think she lives in a dump and therefore
smells bad. What book is she in?
    In what book will you meet Joyce Adams who lives
with Ape and whose best friend is the school janitor?

650. Mrs. Frisby and the Rats of NIMH by Robert C. O'Brien
    In what award-winning book is a colony of rats given
injections to give them longer life and higher intelligence?
    In order to save Jeremy the crow's life, Timothy's
mother gnaws through the string holding him to the
fence. Then just as Dragon the cat leaps, Jeremy
takes flight with the mouse clinging to his back. Name
that book!

651. Island of the Blue Dolphins by Scott O'Dell
    In what book do Karana and her little brother, Ramo,
share their island home with a pack of wild dogs?
    Name the book in which Karana lives on an island by
herself for many years.

652. Sing Down the Moon by Scott O'Dell
    The three Indian girls strike out on stolen horses to
escape the Spaniards who have enslaved them. Name
that book!
    Helping Bright Morning escape the white men, Tall
Boy was badly wounded. Now the Navajo girl's family
has forbidden her to marry a cripple. Can you name this
this book?

653. Gardine vs. Hanover by Joan L. Oppenheimer
    When two single-parent families try to merge into
one big happy family, their oldest children, Jill and
Caroline, won't allow it to happen. Name their story.
    Jill hates her new stepsister, Caroline, and nicknames
her Miz Clean. Caroline doesn't like Jill either, and
calls her the Blue Flash. Soon the girls' mutual hatred
leads to constant fighting that forces their parents to
separate. Name that book!

654. The Way to Satin Shore by Phillipa Pearce
    Until she was ten years old, Kate Tranter always
thought her father had drowned on the day she was
born. In what book does she discover that he is still
alive?

In what book are Kate Tranter and her two brothers abandoned by their father because people think he killed his brother?

655. The Dreadful Future of Blossom Culp by Richard Peck
Only Blossom is brave enough to enter the room where a mysterious blue light pulses. For her efforts she is transported seventy years into the future! Name that book!
Name the book in which Blossom Culp tells her history class a story about a looter who bites off her aunt's ring finger.

656. The Ghost Belonged to Me by Richard Peck
Alexander is sure Blossom Culp is responsible for the puppy and the lighted candle in the barn, but he still wonders about her stories of ghosts. What is the book's title?
In what book do a ghost and a boy in a nightshirt save a streetcar full of passengers from certain death on the trestle bridge?

657. Ghosts I Have Been by Richard Peck
In what book does fourteen-year-old Blossom Culp discover that she truly has the Gift of Second Sight, just like her mother?
Name the book in which Alexander is terrified by the ghost of a servant girl who has hanged herself in Miss Dabney's kitchen.

658. Secrets of the Shopping Mall by Richard Peck
School and normal life become things of the past for Barnie and Teresa after they earn the wrath of the vicious King Kobra gang. Name that book!
To stop the leader of the King Kobra gang from killing a cat, Barnie and Teresa drop a brick on his head. Now the Kobras are after them, in this book called....

659. A Chance Wild Apple by Marian Potter
Maureen McCracken is delighted that Uncle Millard's family is moving nearby, until she meets cousin Skeets. Name that book!
Epitome of Lower Upson, a pedigree bull, is tangled in barbed wire. Unless he is freed he will die, but Maureen is the only witness to his dilemma and she knows he may gore whoever frees him. Name that book!

660. The Girl Who Had No Name by Berniece Rabe
     Because she was the tenth daughter, the name on
     the birth certificate simply said Girl Baby Webster.
     What is the title of her story?
     Her cat's name is Clark Gable, but she herself doesn't
     have a name, and since her mama died, no home either.
     Name that book!

661. Figgs and Phantoms by Ellen Raskin
     In what book will you meet a girl with a father named
     Newton Newton, a mother named Sister, and uncles named
     Truman and Human Pretzel, Romulus, Remus, Kadota,
     and Florence Italy?
     Mona wasn't sure she had really been to Capri until
     she saw the bald spot on Ebenezer Bargain's head.
     Name her story.

662. The Westing Game by Ellen Raskin
     Among the specially selected tenants of Sunset
     Towers apartments are a bookie, a burglar, a bomber,
     and a mistake. Name that book!
     Each pair of people receives ten thousand dollars and
     a different set of clues to try to solve a mystery which
     will give them two hundred million dollars. What book
     are they in?

663. The Girl with the Silver Eyes by Willo Davis Roberts
     In what book will you meet Katie, who is one of the
     September children and who has special powers and
     strange eyes?
     Katie, a ten year old, has a unique way of getting
     rid of babysitters that she doesn't like. In what book
     does she frighten them away by making things move
     without touching them?

664. The Pet-Sitting Peril by Willo Davis Roberts
     In what book does Nick, who is almost twelve, think
     he is too old to be afraid to spend the night by himself
     in an old apartment house, even though the electricity
     is off and the house has almost burned down twice in
     the last two weeks?
     Nick thought his summer job would be boring. Get-
     ting paid to take care of a few cats and dogs was the
     only work the small, almost-twelve-year-old boy could
     find. Name the book where Nick becomes involved in
     arson because of his job.

665. Tarantula and the Red Chigger by Mary Robertson
        Name the book in which the Manning brothers throw
      rocks at Lonnie and Ben, steal their clothes and call
      them "nekkid turtles."
        In what book do Lonnie and Ben get marooned on an
      island because of mean, nasty Leroy and Butchie Man-
      ning?

666. Evy-Ivy-Over by Colby Rodowsky
        Sixth-grader Slug never minded finding treasures
      in garbage cans with her grandmother Gussie, or wear-
      ing other people's discarded clothes, until now. Name
      that book!
        In what book does Slug bring a dead man's shoe to
      school for show-and-tell? It is the shoe her grandfather
      was wearing when he was hit by lightning.

667. Call Me Ruth by Marilyn Sachs
        Ruth's joy at immigrating to America changes to sor-
      row and embarrassment when her father dies and her
      mother is arrested. Can you name this book?
        In what book is Ruth's mother, a Russian immigrant,
      arrested and imprisoned for a week?

668. And Nobody Knew They Were There by Otto Salassi
        On his first day in Louisiana, Jakey Darby has a
      fist fight with his cousin, Hogan McGee, is attacked by
      the killer alligator, Old Smiley, and discovers a secret
      cache of supplies. What book is he in?
        In what book do Hogan and Jakey endure pie-eating
      contests, alligators, and a perilous walk across the
      Mississippi River on a narrow catwalk in order to follow
      nine marines on a secret mission?

669. Roller Skates by Ruth Sawyer
        When Lucinda's parents go to Europe for a year, Lu-
      cinda is left with Miss Peters, thank goodness, instead
      of with proper Aunt Emily. Name that book!
        While Lucinda is staying with Miss Peters in New York
      City, she gets to skate to school every morning. What
      book is she in?

670. My Brother the Thief by Marlene Fanta Shyer
        In what book do the Covellis think that Carolyn, their
      housesitter, took their silver cream pitcher while they
      were on vacation?

Carolyn first suspects that Richard is stealing when she finds two purple jackets hidden under his bed, but their mother won't believe her, in this book called....

671. Welcome Home, Jellybean by Marlene Fanta Shyer
Because everyone who gets on the elevator is pushing a button, Neil's sister, Geraldine, pushes one too. Unfortunately, it's the emergency button that sets off a shrieking alarm. Name the book!
Because thirteen-year-old Geraldine is finally toilet-trained, she can go home and live with her family. Her mother wants her home but Neil, her brother, and her father aren't sure in this book called....

672. Moonshadow of Cherry Mountain by Doris Buchanan Smith
What killed the neighbor's cat? If it is Greg's dog, Moonshadow, the dog will be shot because of the agreement Greg's dad made with the owner of the cat. Name that book!
Greg's dog, Moonshadow, always stays in the house until Clara, Greg's newly adopted sister, arrives. Because she is allergic to dogs, Moonshadow is put outside. That's only one reason Greg doesn't like Clara. Can you name this book?

673. The Bronze Bow by Elizabeth Speare
When Joel is captured by the Romans, Rosh refuses to send his outlaw band to rescue him, so Daniel and nineteen young boys plan to attack the squad of Roman soldiers escorting Joel. Name that book!
Name the book in which Daniel has to give up his life as an outlaw in Rosh's gang because of Leah, his witless sister.

674. The Witch of Blackbird Pond by Elizabeth Speare
When Kit Tyler jumps into the icy Connecticut River to rescue a child's doll, she doesn't realize she will be suspected of being a witch because she can swim. Name that book!
Name the book in which Kit Tyler, a young girl born into wealth and luxury, sits awaiting a trial that may leave her branded on the forehead or minus one ear.

675. The Perilous Road by William O. Steele
When Union soldiers steal his new buckskin shirt,

eleven-year-old Chris Brabson swears he will make a
Yank pay for it. What book is this?
   Chris would rather die than take help from a Yankee,
but the Yankee who saves his life is his own brother,
Jethro. What book are they in?

676. A Walk in Wolf Wood by Mary Stewart
      Margaret and John huddle together in a corner of
the room because a huge, gray wolf is waiting for them
to come out, a wolf who will turn into a man at day-
break. What is the title?
      Two children, Margaret and John, find themselves
transported back in time to the fourteenth century to
help break the spell that turns a man into a wolf every
night. Name that book!

677. Dune Shadow by Nancy Stone
      The sand is killing gardens, crashing buildings
down, and covering whole towns. Serena must get
what's left of her family out before the sand kills them
all. What book is this?
      In this book Serena and her grandmother must live
in the town's bank because sand has destroyed their
house and caused her grandmother's leg to be broken.
Can you give the title?

678. Just an Overnight Guest by Eleanora E. Tate
      Margie isn't sure she can stand to have mean little
Ethel Hardisen stay at her house, even though its supposed to be just for one night. What book is this?
      Margie hates it when her mother gives her old, yellow
dress to Ethel Hardisen, their guest for one night.
Then Margie has to sleep with Ethel! That's when she
learns that Ethel wets the bed, in this book called....

679. The Cay by Theodore Taylor
      All his life Phillip has looked down upon black-skinned
people. Now his life depends upon one named Timothy,
an old West Indian. Name that book!
      There are just two people on the barren little island
when the typhoon hits, an old black man named Timothy
and a white boy named Phillip; with them is a cat named
Stew Cat. Name that book!

680. Dan Alone by John Rowe Townsend
      All Dan has left of his runaway mother is a photograph.

Since no one else wants him, he's headed for an orphanage when he falls in with a gang of thieves who make him part of their family. Name that book!

In what book will you meet a homeless boy named Dan, a gang of crooks who take him into their family, and a girl named Olive?

681. The Loner by Esther Wier

In which book will you find a boy with no name, a strong old woman called Boss, who is 6'2" tall in her boots, and Jup and Juno, two sheepdogs?

David wants to be a sheepherder and he wants Boss to be proud of him. And that means going after the killer grizzly on his own. Name that book!

682. Amos Fortune, Free Man by Elizabeth Yates

Can you name the true story of the African prince At-mun, and his life as a slave in America?

Name the true book in which a seventy-one-year-old former slave sets out with a new wife and child to build his own home and business as a tanner in the 1700's.

683. Child of the Owl by Laurence Yep

Casey doesn't want to live with her Uncle Phil the Pill and he doesn't want her either, because she isn't a good influence on his daughter, Pam-Pam. What is the title?

Only Casey's grandmother, Paw-Paw, knows the identity of the thief who stole her charm and knocked her to the floor, but she won't tell. Name that book!

684. Dragon of the Lost Sea by Laurence Yep

Thorn doesn't know that his rescuer from another beating is really a dragon named Shimmer who is disguised as an old woman. Name the book in which Thorn and Shimmer become friends as they search for a witch named Civet.

A unicorn, a dream pearl, a blue pebble that contains a stolen sea, a boy named Thorn, a princess named Shimmer who isn't human, and a witch named Civet are all found in this exciting book called....

685. Remember Me When I Am Dead by Carol Beach York

Jenny Loring is the only one who doesn't cry at her mother's funeral, because she is sure her mother is coming back. Name that book!

Sara and Jenny like their new stepmother, Margaret, but the shadow of their dead mother seems to hang over the house. What is the title of this book?

CHAPTER VI

EASIER READING

686. **A Storm Without Rain** by Jan Adkins
     Jack Carter falls asleep after digging clams. When
     he awakens, he finds himself trapped on an island of
     lepers and transported through time to the year 1904.
     Name that book!
     If you were the main character in this book, you
     would go back in time and become friends with your
     grandfather. That's what Jack Carter does in this
     book called....

687. **The Black Cauldron** by Lloyd Alexander
     In this second book of the Prydain series, Taran
     and his friends set out to destroy Arawn's cauldron
     where he creates his ghastly warriors, the Cauldron-
     Born. What is the title?
     As Adaon lies dying, he gives a strange brooch to
     Taran, which gives him visions of the future. Name
     that book!

688. **The Book of Three** by Lloyd Alexander
     Impatient for adventure, Taran, Assistant Pig-Keeper,
     finds it when Hen Wen, the most valuable pig in Pry-
     dain, runs away. Can you name this book?
     Name the book in which Taran meets Gurgi--a comical
     half-man, half-beast--who wants to eat him!

689. **The High King** by Lloyd Alexander
     The Huntsmen of Annuvin have stolen Lord Gwydion's
     enchanted sword, Dyrnwyn, and Taran and his compan-
     ions must get it back. Name that book!
     In what book does Princess Eilonwy, armed only with

magic eggs and mushrooms, save Taran from the greedy
Magg?

690. The Kestrel by Lloyd Alexander
    Despite the fact that she is now Queen of Westmark,
    Mickle plans to join the search for Theo--if she can
    find some dirt. Name that book!
    Theo is on his way to aid Queen Augusta when he
    runs into Skeit, a henchman of the evil Cabbarus.
    What book are they in?

691. The Marvelous Misadventures of Sebastian by Lloyd
    Alexander
    When Sebastian's roommate at the Golden Stag Inn
    dumps a bucket of wash water on his head, he is as-
    tonished to discover who he, or rather she, really is!
    What is the title of this book?
    This unemployed fiddler finds himself in one scrape
    after another. Now he has a runaway princess lying
    unconscious at his feet and a murdered innkeeper in
    the stable nearby. Name his story.

692. Taran Wanderer by Lloyd Alexander
    Name the fourth book of the Prydain cycle in which
    Taran travels to the Marshes of Morva to find out who
    he really is.
    The evil wizard Morda changes Fflewddur into a rab-
    bit and Gurgi into a mouse, as Taran awaits his fate in
    terror. Name that book!

693. Westmark by Lloyd Alexander
    Name the book in which the evil prime minister Cab-
    barus tries to kill a young princess by stepping on her
    hands and making her fall down a deep well.
    The King and Queen thought their daughter had
    died years ago. In what book does a boy named Theo
    help them discover that she is alive?

694. The Journey of the Shadow Bairns by Margaret J. An-
    derson
    Arthur and Geoffery Whitcomb sneak Robbie and
    Elspeth MacDonald past the Canadian immigration man
    by hiding them in an iron bathtub in this book called....
    When Elspeth recovers from a five-day illness she
    discovers that her little brother, Robbie, is missing and
    that she's all alone in a new country! Name that book!

695. Night Journeys by Avi
      Instead of capturing the runaway bondsmen and earn-
      ing the reward, twelve-year-old Peter York finds him-
      self adrift in a boat headed toward the deadly Finger
      Falls. Name that book!
      Without thinking, Peter York fires his rifle at the
      escaping girl, and, as she collapses into the river,
      the water turns red with her blood. Can you name
      this book?

696. Shadrach's Crossing by Avi
      The raps on the front door are a warning. They
      mean lights out and no one move until the smugglers
      have finished their work. When Shadrach defies the
      warning, he incurs the wrath of the smugglers' leader.
      Name that book!
      Bootleggers on Lucker's Island are forcing the island-
      ers to help them smuggle liquor. The only islanders
      brave enough to defy them are two young boys, Shad-
      rach and Brian, in this book called....

697. T.H.U.M.B. by T. Ernesto Bethancourt
      The Hippest Underground Marching Band in Brooklyn
      is the creation of Aurelio and Thomas, two high-school
      students. Name the book in which their band performs
      on national television.
      Jimmy the Rat, Charlie Thomas, Che and Fat Albert
      are members of a dreaded gang at Thaddeus Stevens
      High. The other kids call them the Godzillas and avoid
      them whenever possible because their favorite pastime
      is shaking kids down for coins. What book are they
      in?

698. Willow Whip by Irene Bennett Brown
      Willow rides Eagle as fast as she can to get snake-
      bitten Clay to the doctor. Once there, the doctor dis-
      covers Clay's foot has been stepped on by a mule, not
      bitten by a snake. Name that book!
      No work is too hard for Willow. She will do anything
      to help earn money for "The Ranch," anything except
      trap animals for furs. What book is she in?

699. The Court of the Stone Children by Eleanor Cameron
      Name the book in which Nina meets Dominique, a
      strange and beautiful girl, who leads her back in time
      and space to Napoleon's empire.

Was Dominique's father guilty? Only Nina can clear
his name--almost two hundred years after the murder.
Name that book!

700. Behind the Attic Wall by Sylvia Cassedy
Maggie Turner has been thrown out of nine boarding
schools because of poor adjustment. Finally, she is
sent to live with her Aunt Harriet and Aunt Lillian at
the Adelphi Hills Academy where she keeps hearing
voices in the walls. What book is she in?
What book has a girl named Maggie, two dolls named
Timothy John and Miss Christabel, and five imaginary
little girls called the backwoods girls?

701. Shen of the Sea by Arthur Bowie Chrisman
Can you give the title of this collection of Chinese
stories? One story tells how printing was invented by
a small boy who loved jam.
The title story of this collection tells how King Chieh
Chung regained his city and bottled up six water-demons.
Can you name the book?

702. Secret of the Andes by Ann Nolan Clark
In all the eight years of his life, Cusi has never
seen a human being other than Chuto, the old Inca he
lives with high in the mountains. Name his story.
In which book does Cusi, the shepherd boy, wonder
if he might have royal blood because of the golden
plugs he wears in his ears?

703. Hazel Rye by Vera and Bill Cleaver
Her father won't let her have her ears pierced so
they fight for four days. Finally, as a peace offering,
he gives her three acres of land with a dying orange
grove. Her name is the title of this book. What is it?
She's never read an entire book and she can't use a
dictionary. When she fails sixth grade she doesn't care,
until she meets a family whose members read two, sometimes three books at the same time. Her name is the
title of this book. What is it?

704. Queen of Hearts by Vera and Bill Cleaver
When Wilma and Claybrook go to visit Granny, they
find the house closed up and a mysterious shape under
a blanket on the floor. Name that book!

Wilma and her Granny never hit it off well before,
and now after suffering a stroke, Granny seems to have
become a real enemy to Wilma and her little brother.
What book is this?

705.   Hail, Hail Camp Timberwood by Ellen Conford
       Melanie's first time at summer camp looks like it may
be a disaster until she meets Steve. Name that book!
       Summer camp would be fun for Melanie if it weren't
for swimming lessons, a horse with a mind of his own,
and a girl named Ricky. Do you know the title?

706.   Dawn of Fear by Susan Cooper
       When Derek and his friends attack the White Road
gang with mudballs, they aren't prepared for what happens next. What book is this?
       Peter, Derek, and Geoffry were excited when a Ger-
man bomb closed their school and gave them more time
to work on their secret camp. But now the bombs are
coming closer! Name that book!

707.   Greenwitch by Susan Cooper
       Barney's drawing, and Rufus, a dog, are stolen by
the mysterious, Dark man in this book called....
       Great-Uncle Merry knows the forces of the Dark are
at work again when the golden Grail is stolen from the
museum. Name that book!

708.   Over Sea, Under Stone by Susan Cooper
       A secret door behind a wardrobe, a hidden, dusty
attic and an ancient treasure map are the beginnings
of a great adventure for Barney, Simon, and Jane.
What is this book's name?
       Name the first book of a series which tells the eter-
nal story of good vs. evil, involving the grail of King
Arthur, three English school children, and the evil Mr.
Withers.

709.   Enchantress from the Stars by Sylvia Louise Engdahl
       When Alana sneaks into a starship headed for the
planet Andrecia, she doesn't know she will change the
course of history for two different worlds. What is the
name of this book?
       Can the brothers Georyn and Terwyn kill the fire-
belching dragon beyond the Enchanted Forest? And is

it really a dragon? The name of this science-fiction
thriller is....

710. **Hitty, Her First Hundred Years** by Rachel Field
      Phoebe Preble is sure that her doll will keep the
ship **Diana-Kate** from sinking, because her doll is made
of mountain-ash, a special wood that is supposed to be
a lucky charm. What book is this?
      Name the book in which a doll made of mountain-ash
wood becomes shipwrecked on an island with Phoebe,
her owner, and is carried off by natives to become
their heathen idol.

711. **Julie of the Wolves** by Jean Craighead George
      In order to be accepted by Amaroq, the wolf-pack
leader, the Eskimo girl must bite him gently under the
chin. Name this book.
      Julie's only hope of surviving in the Alaskan tundra
is to become friends with a wolf pack. Can you name
this book?

712. **Them That Glitter and Them That Don't** by Bette Greene
      Carol Ann Delaney wants to become famous as Carlotta
Dell, a country western star. Can you name her story?
      Carol Ann's mother is a gypsy fortune-teller, so the
kids at school call Carol Ann "Little Gyp." What book is
she in?

713. **Does This School Have Capital Punishment?** by Nat
      Hentoff
      It was Saddlefield's marijuana, but Sam and Rob got
caught with it, and now they're about to be expelled!
Name that book!
      When Sam and Rob are caught with joints in their
hands, the school director wants them expelled, but
they claim they're innocent in this book called....

714. **Alan and the Animal Kingdom** by Isabelle Holland
      When Alan's Aunt Jessie dies, Alan decides to keep
her death a secret so he can keep his pets, Winchester,
Muff, Alexis, Wallace, and Mr. and Mrs. Gerbil. Name
his story.
      Neighbors, friends, and teachers are all asking about
Aunt Jessie. What they don't know is that she's dead,
and Alan is determined to keep her death a secret.
Name that book!

715. Slake's Limbo by Felice Holman
        In what book does thirteen-year-old Artemis Slake
      share his breakfast each morning with a rat?
        Name the book in which a lonely, outcast teenager
      makes his home in a New York subway tunnel.

716. The Wild Children by Felice Holman
        In what book does Alex, a young Russian boy, go
      downstairs for breakfast and discover that his entire
      family has disappeared?
        Only when Alex climbs on top of a pile of dirty sacks
      for a little rest does he realize that they are really a
      group of children dressed in filthy rags, huddled to-
      gether for warmth. What book are they in?

717. Escape into Daylight by Geoffrey Household
        As Carrie Falconer watches in horror, the old ladder
      on the side of the well breaks and Mike crashes down
      into the black water! Name that book!
        Name the book in which Michael Prowse wakes up to
      discover he has been drugged and kidnapped because he
      happened to recognize a famous movie star.

718. Frozen Fire; A Tale of Courage by James Houston
        When the Mounted Police plane takes off to search for
      Mr. Morgan and Charlie, lost in the frozen Arctic, only
      Matthew knows they are headed in the wrong direction.
      Name that book!
        Seventy-five miles from civilization, in the middle of
      the Canadian Arctic, Kayak and Matthew discover they
      have lost all the gas for their snowmobile. What book
      is this?

719. A Night Without Stars by James Howe
        What book has the following characters: Gotta Lotta
      and Harry Terri, who are nurses, the Mad Bomber and
      the Monster Man, who are patients?
        Maria, in the hospital for heart surgery, is comforted
      by another patient who is so ugly he is called the Mons-
      ter Man. What book are they in?

720. Switching Tracks by Dean Hughes
        Mark Austin didn't know why he got mixed up with
      the old man and his trains, but at least it was a way
      to get money for the video arcade. Name that book!

Name the book in which thirteen-year-old Mark Austin plays "Space Invaders" in order to escape his own thoughts about his father's death.

721. A Stranger Came Ashore by Mollie Hunter
Everyone at Black Ness thought Finn Learson was a survivor from the sunken ship Bergen. But he turns out to be something very different and much more dangerous in this suspenseful book called....
On his death bed, Old Da, Robbie's grandfather, warns him about the stranger Finn Learson. But how can Robbie save his sister when no one will believe him? Name that book!

722. A Girl Called Boy by Belinda Hurmence
Name the book in which a pampered, spoiled black girl is transported back in time to the cruel world of slavery.
Blanche Overtha Yancey is transported back in time by a conjure bird. In what book does she experience, first hand, the life of her slave ancestors?

723. Tough Tiffany by Belinda Hurmence
In what book does a girl named Tiffany make a pickle sandwich with five slices of bread and four kinds of pickles?
Because stingy old Granny Turner doesn't believe in banks, she hides her money at home, but sometimes forgets where. Name the book in which Granny grudgingly gives Tiffany $100.00 for finding her money.

724. Our Eddie by Sulamith Ish-Kishor
When Eddie begins bringing surprise gifts home from the store where he works, the Raphel family suspects nothing--until one night the store manager appears at the door. What is the title?
In what book does Eddie's father refuse to come to the hospital, even though Eddie has only a 50 percent chance of recovery from his operation?

725. Smoky, The Cowhorse by Will James
What book tells the story of a horse, born wild on the range, branded with a "Rocking R," and "broke" by a cowboy named Clint?

Clint, a cowboy, is unconscious because a cow has stepped on him. In what book does his "half-broke" horse carry him back to the corral?

726. Charmed Life by Diana Wynne Jones
When Cat and Gwendolen's parents are swept away in a paddleboat disaster, the two orphans are taken in by Mrs. Sharp, who is a witch. What is the title? In what book does Chrestomanci have Gwendolen spanked with a boot as punishment for using her magic powers in a naughty way?

727. Witch Week by Diana Wynne Jones
At Larwood House, a boarding school, it rains shoes, pens write by themselves, and a teacher flies around on a carpet because someone in the sixth-grade class is a witch! Name that book!
Even though Nan is a descendant of the famous witch Dulcinea Wilkes, she can't get the knack of riding a broom. She always rides upside down and bumps into things in this book called....

728. And Now Miguel by Joseph Krumgold
This book tells about a twelve-year-old boy with only one dream--to go with the shepherds to the Sangre de Cristo mountains. But how can he convince them that he is ready? Name the title.
Even though the teacher is calling him, Miguel Chavez knows that finding the lost sheep is more important than school. What book is he in?

729. A Ring of Endless Light by Madeleine L'Engle
Name the book in which Vicky discovers that her old boyfriend, Zachary, is to blame for Commander Rodney's death.
There are three boys in Vicky's life, Leo, Zachary and Adam, and a dolphin named Basil. What is the title of her story?

730. A Wrinkle in Time by Madeleine L'Engle
In what book do Mrs. Whatsit, Mrs. Who, and Mrs. Which help Meg and Charles Wallace find their father who disappeared from this planet?
On the planet Camazotz everyone is programmed to obey the mysterious "It" who lives in the Central Central Intelligence Center. Name that book!

731. The Ghost of Thomas Kempe by Penelope Lively
        James Harrison didn't believe in ghosts, until one
      takes him on as his apprentice and even advertises on
      the town's notice board! What is the title of this book?
        In what book does James Harrison hire Bert Ellison
      to exorcise a ghost who is getting James in a lot of
      trouble?

732. Taking Care of Terrific by Lois Lowry
        Fourteen-year-old Enid has been arrested for kid-
      napping and theft. As she waits for the legal system
      to decide her fate, she begins to tell the reader the
      story of her arrest in this book called....
        Name the book that is full of people with secret
      identities, such as Tom Terrific, Cynthia Crowley, the
      Hawk, and General Seth Sandroff.

733. Turkeylegs Thompson by Jean McCord
        Betty Ann wants only two things--a watch and a
      bicycle--but all she has is her little brother and sister
      to take care of and an insulting nickname. Name her
      story.
        On the day she skips school with her little brother,
      this tough teenager also steals a new bicycle that seems
      to be meant for her. Her name is the title of the book.
      Do you know it?

734. Invincible Louisa by Cornelia Meigs
        This is the true life story of the author of LITTLE
      WOMEN, the strong and adventurous Louisa May Alcott.
      What is the title?
        When Bronson Alcott tried to sell one of his daughter
      Louisa's stories, the editor told him Louisa would never
      be a writer. Can you name this biography?

735. Rascal by Sterling North
        Eleven-year-old Sterling has pet skunks, woodchucks,
      a crow, many cats, and a Saint Bernard, but this true
      book is about his very special pet raccoon that he raises
      from a kit. What is the title?
        Name the book in which a pet raccoon learns the hard
      way that he can't wash his sugar lump in his milk before
      he eats it.

736. Just Good Friends by Jane O'Connor
        Joss Longman wanted to attract handsome Twig

Lorimer's attention, but stabbing her hand and passing out wasn't what she had in mind. Name that book!

When Joss sees her mother crying and her college-professor father downtown with a pretty student, she assumes her parents will be getting a divorce in this book called....

737. Child of Fire by Scott O'Dell
This action-filled story is told by Parole Officer Ben Delaney, who, with over forty delinquent boys to over-see, finds himself involved in everything from bullfights to drug smuggling. Name that book!

We first meet sixteen-year-old Manuel Castillo as he jumps into the bullring, drops to his knees and faces a 1000-pound bull. Can you name this book?

738. And You Give Me a Pain, Elaine by Stella Pevsner
In what book is Andrea put in charge of special effects for the school play, "Count Dracula"?

It isn't fair that Andrea's parents pay so much attention to her bratty older sister, Elaine, and so little to her. And now Elaine has gained even more attention by running away to Arizona. What is the title?

739. Alan Mendelsohn, the Boy From Mars by Daniel Manus Pinkwater
Cigar smoking won't make you sick if you chew bubble gum at the same time. That's just one lesson Leonard Neeble learns from his best friend. What book is he in?

When Leonard and Alan buy Samuel Klugarsh's Mind Control Course for $24.00, they are sure they have been swindled, until it works! Name that book!

740. Summer of the Monkeys by Wilson Rawls
Jay and his hound, Rowdy, live a carefree life in the Ozark foothills of northeastern Oklahoma territory, until the day Rowdy trees a monkey. Name that book!

In the Ozark river bottoms Jay and Rowdy had al-ways watched out for snakes and wild hogs, but they never thought they would be attacked by monkeys! What is the title?

741. Where the Red Fern Grows by Wilson Rawls
After two years of saving and a thirty-mile walk, Billy Colman finally picks up his coon-hound pups,

but gets beaten up and laughed at, too. Name his
story.
    Old Dan has the strength and courage, and Little
Ann, the brains. Together they become the best coon-
hound team in the Ozark hills. What book are they in?

742. The Horsecatcher by Mari Sandoz
    While trying to capture the colt with the bear-shaped
marking on his side, Young Elk becomes trapped deep
inside enemy territory. Name that book!
    Young Elk's warrior name is Kiowa Killer, but it is
a name he doesn't want to live up to. What book is he
in?

743. Kidnapping Mr. Tubbs by Don Schellie
    In what book will you find two teenagers, a bassett
hound named Gwendolyn, a saddle, and a runaway from
a rest home, all crammed in an ancient Volkswagen with
a horn that won't stop blowing?
    Stopped at the side of the road by motorcycle toughs,
A.J. tries to scare them with Gwendolyn, Eloise's dog,
but the dog just wags her tail and makes a puddle.
What book is this?

744. The Sign of the Beaver by Elizabeth Speare
    When Matt throws the dead rabbit in the bear's face,
he distracts the bear and gives Attean a chance to kill
it. Name that book!
    The Indian boy Attean saves Matt's life after Matt is
attacked by a swarm of bees, in this book called....

745. Heidi by Johanna Spyri
    Everyone in the village is frightened of the Alm-
Uncle, with his long beard, bushy eyebrows, and fierce
eyes. Name the book in which his five-year-old granddaughter is taken up the mountain to live with him.
    This book is named after a girl who goes to live on
a mountain with her grandfather, and whose best friend
is Peter, the goatherd. Do you know the title?

746. Roll of Thunder, Hear My Cry by Mildred Taylor
    In this book which takes place in the 1930's, Cassie's
parents arrange a shopping cooperative to boycott a
store run by the Wallaces, men who have mistreated
blacks. What is the title?

In Mississippi in 1933 Cassie finds out that black
students only get the school books that white students
have already worn out. What book is this?

747. Jasmin by Jan Truss
        In what book will you find a runaway girl with a
name fit for a queen, her retarded brother, and a
ruined science-fair project?
        Jasmin Marie Antoinette Stalke is tired of being the
oldest child in her strange family and having to take
care of her six little brothers and sisters, so she runs
away to live in the wilderness. Name that book!

748. Building Blocks by Cynthia Voigt
        Brann crawls inside his block fortress and falls
asleep. When he awakens he meets a ten year old who
turns out to be his father! Name that book!
        The wooden blocks were made by Uncle Andrew for
Brann's father. Now Brann has them and he discovers
that they have a special power. What book is this?

749. When No One Was Looking by Rosemary Wells
        Julia Redmond and Kathy Bardy have been best
friends since first grade, the kind of best friends who
will do anything for each other, even murder. Name
that book!
        Kathy Bardy is on her way to becoming a profes-
sional tennis player. The only things that stand in her
way are her temper and a girl named Ruth Gumm. What
is the title?

750. The Watch House by Robert Westall
        While dusting the relics in the long white building,
Anne watches in horror as ghostly writing, pleading for
help, appears in the dust! Name that book!
        Out of hundreds of graves, the mangy dog only digs
at five--the graves of young men drowned in the river
between October 1854 and July 1855. Name this ghostly
book!

751. Blodwen and the Guardians by David Wiseman
        In what book does Mr. Lewis tell Blodwen not to
walk down Mow Grove, because Sally Webster, the last
person to do so, has never been right in the head since
she walked there?
        The workers building the motorway through Mow

Grove have never had so much bad luck on the job
before. They blame it on Gremlins but it's really the
Guardians, in this book called....

752. Shadow of a Bull by Maia Wojciechowska
     How could the son of the bravest man who ever lived
     be a coward? Manolo decides he must hide his fear un-
     til he learns to be brave. Name that book!
     The whole town of Arcangel is waiting for Manolo to
     grow up and become a famous bullfighter like his father,
     but Manolo knows one thing they don't--he isn't brave
     enough. What is the title of this book?

ADVANCED READING

753. Watership Down by Richard Adams
     Bigwig is brave and strong but bossy, Hazel is a
     true leader, and his brother, Fiver, can see into the
     future. They are all characters in a book called....
     Is the sleek, well-fed rabbit named Cowslip a friend
     or an enemy? No one knows until Bigwig faces an
     agonizing death. Name that book!

754. Little Men by Louisa May Alcott
     To cure Nat of his habit of fibbing, Mr. Bhaer tries a
     strange punishment: Nat must whip Mr. Bhaer with the
     rod each time he, Nat, lies. Can you name this book?
     When smoking, drinking, and gambling lead to a
     dangerous fire at Plumfield, Mr. Bhaer decides Dan, the
     new boy, must leave. Name that book!

755. Little Women by Louisa May Alcott
     To help her sick father, Jo March sells her beautiful,
     long, red hair for twenty-five dollars. What book is
     she in?
     Name the book in which Beth March receives a piano
     from Mr. Laurence, her next door neighbor, in return
     for a pair of handmade shoes.

756. Anna to the Infinite Power by Mildred Ames
     Anna Zimmerman Hart can't believe her eyes. There,
     browsing through a rack of clothes at the Greenwich
     Department Store, is her exact double! Name that book!
     Food is scarce. That's why it's so important that the

replicator, a machine that can produce food from air, is
completed. In what book does Anna Zimmerman Hart
discover that some people will do anything to see that
the machine is finished?

757. Dear Lola: Or How to Build Your Own Family by Judie
       Angell
            Al-Willie, Annie, James, Edmund, Ben, and Lola are
       orphans who decide not to let any family adopt just one
       of them--it's all or none. In what book do they each
       devise their own special method to discourage any family
       that tries?
            Edmund Beniker and his new friend Orie Stamwick
       love cats. They decide to have a cat birthday party in
       the kindergarten classroom but their seven, very angry
       cats tear the room apart. What is this book called?

758. Waterless Mountain by Laura Adams Armer
            When the trader's car won't start, Younger Brother
       knows what to do. He spits juniper juice on it! What
       book is this?
            Younger Brother is an eight-year-old Navajo boy. In
       what book does he dream he flies up to the sky and
       plays with the star children?

759. Kept in the Dark by Nina Bawden
            Their grandparents don't want Noel, Clara, and
       Bosie to live with them, so things don't go very well
       until the mysterious and evil relative, David, comes to
       stay. Name that book!
            Name the book in which Bosie, short for Ambrose,
       breaks into his headmaster's office to erase some names
       from the Black Book.

760. The Dark Frigate by Charles Boardman Hawes
            When the Old One and his pirate gang capture the
       Rose of Devon, young Phil Marsham is given a choice--
       join the pirate gang or die! Name that book!
            Name the book in which Phil Marsham saves Martin
       Barwick from drowning by dragging him from the sea
       by the hair of his head, back aboard the Rose of Devon.

761. A String in the Harp by Nancy Bond
            Every time Peter Morgan holds the strange key he
       found on the beach in Wales, it vibrates with sound and

takes him back to another time. In what book does this happen?

Aneirin and Taliesen lived in the sixth century, but Peter Morgan from the twentieth century knows them well. In fact, he wears the tuning key to Taliesen's harp around his neck. Name that book!

762. The Moves Make the Man by Bruce Brooks

Jerome Foxworthy takes Home Ec because he needs to learn how to cook nutritious meals for his brothers, but the first thing he learns to make is Mock-Apple Pie which is mostly Ritz crackers. What book is he in?

In what book does Bix challenge his stepfather to a game of basketball? If Bix wins, he gets to visit his mother in the mental hospital.

763. Surrogate Sister by Eve Bunting

Cassie usually gives her mom a bottle of Arpège for Mother's Day, but this year she doesn't because her mother has done something unforgivable. This book is called....

Cassie has never seen Mr. X, but he's still going to be the father of her brother! Name that book!

764. Tawny by Chas Carner

In what book is Trey Landry's twin brother, Troy, shot by poachers?

Trey enjoys all the attention his pet deer is getting, until someone asks when he will set her free. Name that book!

765. A Hero Ain't Nothing But a Sandwich by Alice Childress

Benjie Johnson says he's not hooked. He can kick the drug habit anytime he wants to, but he has plenty of time. After all, he's only thirteen. Name that book!

When Benjie steals his stepfather's coat for drug money, Butler feels like killing him, and soon he has a chance as Benjie dangles from the roof, begging Butler to let him drop. What book is this?

766. Where the Lilies Bloom by Vera and Bill Cleaver

In what book does Mary Call save a man's life with the onion cure--that is, covering him in gooey fried onions from head to foot?

When Mr. and Mrs. Connell come to pay a visit to

Roy Luther, Mary Call and Romey dare not tell them that
he is not sick but dead. What book is this?

767. The Curse of the Moonraker by Eth Clifford
    In this exciting adventure, a ship carrying eighty-
three passengers is pulled into a sea cavern and smashed
to bits, leaving only ten survivors. Name that book!
    Unconscious in the midst of a shipwreck, Catlow
Rider feels someone steal his greenstone jade amulet
from his neck--the amulet that is supposed to keep him
safe from harm. What is the title?

768. My Brother Sam Is Dead by James Lincoln and Christo-
    pher Collier
    Even though Tim's brother Sam has run off to fight
the British, the war doesn't seem real until Tim sees a
rebel officer holding a sword to his father's stomach.
Name that book!
    Should Tim be a Tory like his parents or a Rebel
like his brother Sam? The Revolutionary War comes to
life in this book called....

769. War Comes to Willy Freeman by James Lincoln and Chris-
    topher Collier
    Willy watches as the British soldiers kill everyone at
Fort Griswold, then closes her eyes. When she opens
them, in front of her is a British soldier holding a
bloody bayonet. Name that book!
    After witnessing her father's death in a Revolutionary
War battle and discovering that her mother is missing,
Wilhelmina Freeman, disguised as a boy, sets off to
find her. What book is this?

770. The Winter Hero by James Lincoln and Christopher
    Collier
    In what book is Justin's hot-tempered brother-in-law,
Peter, ready to shoot the sheriff because he tries to
take the family's oxen?
    What book tells the exciting story of Shays' Rebellion
in Massachusetts during the winter of 1786-1787?

771. The Dark Is Rising by Susan Cooper
    In this second book of the series, Will must find the
six magical signs which will help the Old Ones in their
last battle. Can you name the book?

In what book does eleven-year-old Will Stanton discover he is not an ordinary boy but an immortal being
with a special and very dangerous mission?

772. **The Grey King** by Susan Cooper
         In this fourth book of a series, Will Stanton is sent
to Wales to recover from an illness and finds Bran, the
albino boy with the golden eyes. Name that book!
         In which book does Will first see the milgwn, huge
grey foxes who are agents of the Dark?

773. **Seaward** by Susan Cooper
         Cally and Westerly are being chased by the Stonecut-
ter, a creature whose touch turns humans into stone!
Name that book!
         Just before Westerly's mother is killed, she shows
him how to enter another land and instructs him to trust
only three people. One of the three is a man with eyes
like an owl. What is the title of this book?

774. **Silver on the Tree** by Susan Cooper
         Can you name the last book of a series set in Scot-
land in which the forces of Light and Dark come together
in a final thunderous battle?
         In this adventure Will and Bran are chased by a
nightmarish skeleton horse. Name that book!

775. **The Bumblebee Flies Anyway** by Robert Cormier
         Name the book in which the main character lives in a
place called the Complex, is under the control of the
Hangman, and receives something he calls the merchan-
dise.
         Name the book in which sixteen-year-old Barney Snow
voluntarily undergoes experiments to blot out his short-
term memory.

776. **Robinson Crusoe** by Daniel Defoe
         This is the tale of a shipwrecked man who lived for
twenty-eight years, two months, and nineteen days on
an island before being rescued. Can you name this
book?
         After many years alone on the island, this man saves
a native from cannibals and gains a faithful servant.
The man's name is the title of the book. What is it?

777. A Christmas Carol by Charles Dickens
      The sign over the warehouse that says "Scrooge
and Marley" is wrong, because Marley died seven years
before this story begins. What is the title?
      Three spirits visit this mean, stingy old man at
Christmas time to convince him to change his ways before it is too late. Name that book!

778. To Take a Dare by Crescent Dragonwagon and Paul
Zindel
      In what book do you meet runaway Chrysta, who,
although only sixteen, takes in twelve-year-old Dare?
      Chrysta takes in twelve-year-old, homeless Dare,
and he repays her kindness by pulling a knife on her
in this book called....

779. Incident at Hawk's Hill by Allan W. Eckert
      In what book would you find a female badger lying
in agony, her foot caught in a trap, as she hears the
desperate whining of her starving pups in the den
nearby?
      Hurt and lost in the midst of a thunderstorm, Ben
MacDonald finds refuge in a badger's burrow. What
happens when the badger returns is an amazing story,
based on a real event. Name that book!

780. Johnny Tremain by Esther Forbes
      Johnny is the proudest and best silversmith appren-
tice in Boston, until an accident leaves his right hand
crippled. Name his story.
      In what book does Johnny have to learn to chop
wood with his left hand so he can take part in the Boston Tea Party along with Paul Revere?

781. The Slave Dancer by Paula Fox
      Because thirteen-year-old Jesse Bollier could play
the fife, he was kidnapped and made to play on a slav-
ing ship. Name his story.
      The Moonlight is a ship whose cargo is ninety-eight
human beings. This book tells the story of a boy made
to play music for their exercise. Its title is....

782. The Talking Earth by Jean Craighead George
      Because the Indian girl Billie Wind is a doubter, she
is sent alone into the Everglades to find the Great Ser-
pent, in this book called....

As fire sweeps the island, Billie Wind knows the only
place she can survive is in a cave deep inside a sink-
hole. Name that book!

783. The Edge of the World by John Gordon
    Kit and Tekker's backs are against the impenetrable
glass wall and the hideous horse-head things are coming
closer and closer! Name that book!
    In what book do Kit and Tekker risk their lives to
save Dan, who is dying because one of evil Ma Grist's
friends touched him?

784. Adam of the Road by Elizabeth Janet Gray
    After five long months in St. Alban's Abbey school,
Adam can hardly believe that his father, Roger the
minstrel, has come to take him to London. Name that
book!
    In which book does Roger the minstrel tell his son
that he has lost all his money, and even his horse,
gambling?

785. Summer of My German Soldier by Bette Greene
    Because twelve-year-old Patty Bergen helped a Ger-
man prisoner of war escape, she may be tried for trea-
son by the U. S. Government. Name that book!
    Name the book in which a cheap, glass brooch helps
Anton escape from a prisoner-of-war camp in Jenkins-
ville, Arkansas.

786. The House of Dies Drear by Virginia Hamilton
    Thomas doesn't know if his new home is haunted, but
he does know it is full of secret passageways and tun-
nels that date back to before the Civil War. Name that
book!
    In what book do Thomas Small and his father find
unbelievable treasures in an underground cavern?

787. M.C. Higgins, the Great by Virginia Hamilton
    The only way to escape the menacing spoil heap
that hangs over their home is for Mama to become a singing star. So dreams Mayo Cornelius, the main character
of the book called....
    Name the book in which Mayo Cornelius leads Lur-
hetta into a twelve-foot water tunnel and then discovers
that she can't swim!

788. The Planet of Junior Brown by Virginia Hamilton
      In what book does a boy play a piano that makes no
      sound and take his music lessons from a crazy woman?
      In what book do two boys spend almost all semester
      hiding in a secret room in their school that contains a
      working model of the solar system?

789. Sweet Whispers Brother Rush by Virginia Hamilton
      Dab, Tree's brother, suffers from porphyric, a
      disease that is so painful he often can't get out of bed.
      What book are they in?
      In what book does Miss Pricherd get a terrible shock
      when she opens Tree's closet door and sees a ghost
      standing through the middle of a table?

790. Willie Bea and the Time the Martians Landed by Virginia
      Hamilton
      In what book does beautiful Aunt Leah give Willie
      Bea the most wonderful Halloween costume in the world?
      On Halloween night, Toughy and Willie Bea climb on
      their stilts and go looking for invaders from outer space.
      What book are they in?

791. Anpao: An American Indian Odyssey by Jamake High-
      water
      One Indian twin talks and acts normally, the other
      is what is called "contrary." He says the opposite of
      what he means; even his name is spelled backward.
      They are characters in what book?
      According to Indian legend, his name means the
      Dawn. His mother is an Indian and his father is the
      sun in the sky. The name of his story is....

792. The Outsiders by S.E. Hinton
      Ponyboy thinks things could never get worse after
      his older brother hits him, but now Ponyboy and Johnny
      are running away from a murder rap. Name that book!
      Darry, Sodapop, and Ponyboy Curtis are Greasers,
      kids from the wrong side of town. Name the book that
      tells their story of trying to stay together in the midst
      of rumbles, switchblades, fast cars, and death.

793. Tex by S.E. Hinton
      The greatest love in fifteen-year-old Texas McCormick's
      life is his horse, Negrito. In what book does his older
      brother, Mace, sell Negrito to pay the bills?

Why is Tex the next-to-the most swatted kid in
school? Because he pulls tricks like gluing explosive
caps on the typewriter keys before test day. Name
that book!

794. The Empty House by Isabelle Holland
In what book will you find a father jailed for fraud
and two strange women, whose hero is someone they
call "the red knight"?
Just before Betsy's father is taken to jail, he slips
her something to keep for him--five $1000.00 bills!
Name that book!

795. Across Five Aprils by Irene Hunt
When Jethro's sister, Mary, is killed because of a
drunken boy named Travis Burdow, Jethro cannot understand why his father wants to stop the crowd from
lynching Burdow. Name that book!
In what book does eleven-year-old Jethro receive a
letter from Abraham Lincoln about Union Army deserters?

796. Up a Road Slowly by Irene Hunt
Name the book in which Julie and Chris discover the
real meaning of their Uncle Haskell's golf bag and his
private graveyard.
Because Julie won't invite Aggie Kilpin, the smelliest
girl in school, to her birthday party, her Aunt Cordelia
makes her cancel it. Name that book!

797. Tancy by Belinda Hurmence
As soon as she earns her first dollar, this newly
freed slave girl sets out to find Lucy, her mother.
What book is she in?
This slave girl learns that her master is also her
father, and for that reason her mother was sold before
the girl was two years old. Her name is the book's
title. Do you know it?

798. Archer's Goon by Diana Wynne Jones
Name the book in which seven powerful wizards vie
for the 2000 words that Quentin Sykes writes each
month.
In what book do you meet a large creature called a
goon who is not as stupid as he first appears to be?

799. Rifles for Watie by Harold Keith
        This book tells the story of sixteen-year-old Jeff
        Bussey, who left home to join the Union Army and re-
        turned after four years, a man. What is the title?
        When Sparrow the cook is found with a knife in his
        back, Jeff knows Captain Clardy is responsible, and he
        fears that he may be next. Name that book!

800. The Trumpeter of Krakow by Eric Kelly
        Accused of being witches and wizards, Joseph Char-
        netski and his family face death in fifteenth-century
        Poland. Name that book!
        Elzbietka thinks her Uncle Kreutz is possessed, but
        no one knows by whom, except the evil student Johann
        Tring. What is the title of this book?

801. When Hitler Stole Pink Rabbit by Judith Kerr
        What book tells of Anna and her Jewish family's es-
        caping Germany to Switzerland just before the elections
        that put Hitler in power?
        This book tells the story of Anna and her family's
        escape from Nazi Germany to Switzerland, then France,
        then England. Based on the author's true experience,
        its title is....

802. Dinky Hocker Shoots Smack! by M.E. Kerr
        The reason her cousin is so fat, Natalia tells Tucker,
        is that she eats in every restaurant in the neighbor-
        hood every afternoon. What book are these three teen-
        agers in?
        In what book is Susan Hocker given a Weight Watch-
        ers Cook Book for Christmas?

803. Is That You, Miss Blue? by M.E. Kerr
        In which book does Flanders receive roses with a
        note saying, "Don't ever change," from a blind date
        who has never seen her?
        Because Agnes Thatcher is beautiful and deaf, the
        Charles School faculty believe she is an angel--but her
        friends know better! Name that book!

804. The Road From Home: The Story of an Armenian Girl
        by David Kherdian
        In 1915 Turkey decided to do away with every Ar-
        menian in the country. Name the true story of Veron

Dumehjian, a young Armenian girl who survived the
holocaust.
When cholera spread through the Armenian refugee
camp, Veron lost her brothers and then her mother.
Name this biography.

805. The Griffin Legacy by Jan O'Donnell Klaveness
Seth Howes died thinking that his wife, Lucy Griffin,
betrayed him. One hundred and fifty years after his
death, his ghost still appears, in this book called....
Grandma wants Amy to help Lucy Griffin, but Lucy
is a ghost, and Amy isn't sure what kind of help she
needs. Can you name that book?

806. A Swiftly Tilting Planet by Madeleine L'Engle
In this science-fiction adventure, fifteen-year-old
Charles Wallace is called upon to stop a crazy South
American dictator from destroying the universe. Name
that book!
A fifteen-year-old boy with extraordinary powers and
a magnificent unicorn named Gaudior set out to save the
universe from nuclear war in this book called....

807. A Wind in the Door by Madeleine L'Engle
Cosmic screams, rips in the galaxy, dragon droppings,
and disappearing school principals--find them all with
Meg, Calvin, and Charles Wallace in a science-fiction
book called....
In this book, Charles Wallace begins first grade and
gets beaten up almost every day. All seems hopeless
until a strange teacher named Blajeny appears in the
meadow. Name that book!

808. Carry On, Mr. Bowditch by Jean Lee Latham
In this true story, Nat dreams of going to Harvard
to study, but instead finds himself signed over by his
father to be an indentured servant for nine years.
Name that book!
Can you name the biography of a sea captain who
quit school at ten, taught himself Latin, French, and
Spanish, became an excellent mathematician, and wrote
a book on navigation that saved the lives of many sail-
ors?

809. The Tombs of Atuan by Ursula K. LeGuin

In what book does Arha imprison a wizard in the
Great Treasury under the tombs?
Arha faithfully serves her masters until a thief enters the tombs, searching for their greatest treasure,
the broken ring of Ereth-Akbe. Name that book!

810. Young Fu of the Upper Yangtze by Elizabeth Lewis
In what book does a young Chinese apprentice get
his first look at a foreigner and decide that, although
he was ugly, he was probably harmless?
What book tells of China in the early 1900's when
girls' feet were still bound, beggars deliberately crippled themselves, and soldiers shot coolies for refusing
to carry their loads?

811. The Call of the Wild by Jack London
This is the story of Buck, half-St. Bernard/half-
Shepherd, who is stolen from his California home to
work as a sled-dog in the Klondike. What is the title?
In which book do John Thornton and the half-dead
dog, Buck, watch as an overloaded sled, three foolish
people, and four of Buck's husky companions disappear
beneath the ice of the Yukon River?

812. The Root Cellar by Janet Lunn
Rose works hard for the blacksmith, but when he
refuses to pay her, she steals from him. What book is
she in?
Newly orphaned Rose is shipped off to stay with Aunt
Nan in her old farmhouse where she meets a ghost that
calls her by name. What book is she in?

813. The Haunting by Margaret Mahy
A Scholar magician is a powerful worker of magic.
Name the book in which one of the Scholar girls is a
magician with fantastic powers that she misuses by setting her sister Elizabeth's hair on fire. What book is
this?
One day a young boy sees a ghost who tells him that
Barnaby is dead. When the boy hears this message he
faints, because his name is Barnaby Palmer and he is
sure the ghost is talking about him. Name that book!

814. Taking Terri Mueller by Norma Fox Mazer
In what book does Terri discover that her father

has a reason other than his wandering feet for moving
every eight months?

Terri has always been told that her mother died
when Terri was four. In what book does she discover
that her parents were divorced when she was five?

815. The Blue Sword by Robin McKinley
Harry Crewe can't wait to see a Free Hillfolk. Ru-
mor has it that they are giants with one eye and magic
powers! Name that book!

In what book does Harimad'sol battle the not-quite-
human Thurra and his fanged white stallion?

816. The Hero and the Crown by Robin McKinley
Aerin-sol, the Dragon-Killer, has slain many, many
dragons, most of them no bigger than a dog. Now she
must fight Maur, the Black Dragon, whose teeth are as
long as a horse's leg! Name that book!

As revenge for Aerin cutting off her long eyelashes,
Galanna goads Aerin into eating Sukra. One leaf from
this special tree gives super-human strength to someone
of royal blood, but it may be deadly to Aerin, whose
mother was a witchwoman, not royalty. What book are
they in?

817. Gay-Neck; The Story of a Pigeon by Dhan Gopal Mu-
kerji
What book tells the exciting story of a clever carrier
pigeon who served in World War I?

In what book does a pigeon tell his own story of
flying with geese and swifts and of the terrible dangers
of eagles, owls, and weasels?

818. The Case of the Baker Street Irregular by Robert New-
man
In what book does Andrew work for Mr. Sherlock
Holmes without even knowing it?

What book tells of how Andrew helped the most famous detective in all of England, Sherlock Holmes, and
how Mr. Holmes helped Andrew find out who he was?

819. Z for Zachariah by Robert C. O'Brien
What would it be like to be the only person left on
earth? After the war, sixteen-year-old Ann Burden is
sure she is completely alone ... until she sees smoke
in the distance. Name that book!

In what book do a teenage girl and a New York scientist team up to try to survive in the aftermath of a nuclear war?

820. The King's Fifth by Scott O'Dell
What book tells of a young Spanish mapmaker who is on trial for hiding a treasure of gold from the King of Spain?
In what book does a young mapmaker travel with Captain Mendoza to discover the Grand Canyon, the Colorado River, and the thing Mendoza will kill for-- gold?

821. Zia by Scott O'Dell
When Zia and Mando are captured by whalers and made to work on their ship, they decide to take their chances with the sharks in order to escape. Name that book!
Name the book in which a fourteen-year-old Indian girl is jailed for helping her people run away from the Spanish mission in California.

822. Playing Beatie Bow by Ruth Park
Abigail Kirk knows that Judah Bow will die if he sails on the ship The Brothers, but will she be able to travel 100 years back through time to warn him? This book is called....
In what book does fourteen-year-old Abigail Kirk find herself transported back in time, where she falls in love with Judah Bow?

823. Jacob Have I Loved by Katherine Paterson
Louise Bradshaw, the elder twin by a few minutes, is born strong and healthy, but from the moment her frail and gifted sister, Caroline, is born, Louise is almost forgotten. What book is this?
When Louise goes to Auntie Braxton's to return a cat, she discovers the old woman's body on the floor, with cats crawling all over her. Name that book!

824. Are You in the House Alone? by Richard Peck
Gail knows who is sending her love notes, but she's baffled when she starts finding ugly, threatening notes in her locker. What book is she in?
Gail has always enjoyed her Saturday-night babysitting

job at Mrs. Montgomery's, until someone starts scaring
her with threatening phone calls. Name that book!

825. Don't Look and It Won't Hurt by Richard Peck
      In what book does Carol learn that the stranger in
      the park who gives her two quarters for cold drinks is
      her father?
      Carol's first date with Jerry turns into a disaster
      when someone tries to run them off the road. What book
      is this?

826. Nobody Else Can Walk It For You by P.J. Petersen
      It's a camper's worst nightmare come true for Laura
      and her Y youth group when they're attacked by a
      motorcycle gang in this book called....
      In what book does Brian try to smash Laura in the
      face with a rock as she bends over him to see if his leg
      is broken?

827. The Watcher in the Garden by Joan Phipson
      Old Mr. Lovett is blind. He thinks nothing can hurt
      him if he stays in his garden, but Catherine knows he
      is wrong. She can sense someone waiting in the garden,
      someone who wants the old man dead. What book is this?
      Terry and Catherine hate each other at first sight.
      After Terry tries to run her down with his motorcycle,
      they discover that they can read each other's minds.
      What book are they in?

828. The Upstairs Room by Johanna Reiss
      In what book do Annie and Sini hide from the Nazis
      for two years, with the Oosterveld family in Holland?
      When Johan goes into hiding, Dientje is too frightened
      to keep the two Jewish girls at home, so she takes them
      back to the Hannink's cave. What book are they in?

829. On the Ropes by Otto Salassi
      In what book will you meet the Masked Marvel, a
      wrestler, who never lets anyone see his face, not even
      his intended?
      Name the book in which something called Slick-ums
      is used to defeat the Angel of Sorrow and save the
      Gain's Arena and Wrestling Academy.

830. IOU's by Ouida Sebestyen
      Name the book in which a little girl destroys Stowe

Garrett's first and only $100.00 bill because she thinks
it isn't real.

Stowe Garrett saves for a long time, until he has
enough money to have the bank exchange it for a $100.00
bill. His next problem is to find a safe place to keep
it. In what book does he come up with what he thinks
is the perfect solution?

831. Upon the Head of a Goat by Aranka Siegal
What is the title of nine-year-old Piri's true story
of her experience as a Jew in Nazi Hungary?

After the Germans take over her town, Jews have to
wear the star of David, and soon Piri and her family are
forced into a ghetto to live. Name this biography.

832. Fingers by William Sleator
Humphrey is making a comeback as a concert pianist,
thanks to newly written music by a Gypsy composer who
happens to be dead! Name that book!

The hands of Gypsy pianist Laszlo Magyar disappeared after his death, but Sam thinks he has just discovered them on his brother's bed, in this book called....

833. House of Stairs by William Sleator
In which book are five sixteen-year-old orphans
blindfolded and taken to a strange place made entirely
of stairs?

Name the science-fiction book which tells the story
of five teenagers who are placed in a maze of stairs as
a scientific experiment.

834. Interstellar Pig by William Sleator
Name the book in which Ted Martin tries to beat
Zena, Manny, and Joe to the Piggy.

The scratches on the wall of Ted's room are really
a map that shows where the Piggy is hidden. Can you
name that book?

835. Journey Outside by Mary Q. Steele
In order to prove to Grandfather that their rafts go
nowhere, Dilar jumps off onto a cavern ledge and finds
himself surrounded by fierce creatures with long yellow
teeth and red eyes. What is the title?

When Dilar sees the bloody places in the snow, he
wonders if Wingo is really kind or if he has trapped Dilar
for the tigers. Name that book!

836. Treasure Island by Robert Louis Stevenson
     Name the exciting story of Jim Hawkins who sails as
     cabin-boy on the Hispaniola and finds adventure and
     danger on the high seas.
         Squire Trelawney and Dr. Livesay think they have
     the best ship's crew possible, until Jim overhears plans
     for mutiny while he is hidden in an apple barrel. Name
     that book!

837. The Sodbuster Venture by Charlene Joy Talbot
     A sodbuster's life is hard; there is little food and
     much sickness. Maud tends Mr. Nelson but the doctor
     arrives too late. He thinks Mr. Nelson is Maud's hus-
     band, even though she is only thirteen. Can you name
     that book?
         Maud and Belle are determined to spend the year as
     sodbusters. In store for them are a grasshopper plague,
     blizzards, cattle stampedes, drunken neighbors, and the
     mysterious Mr. Southern. What book are they in?

838. The Dark Didn't Catch Me by Crystal Thrasher
     When Seely almost steps on some snakes, her screams
     cause her little brother, Jamie, to burn himself with hot
     gravy. Later in this book, she thinks she causes his
     death. What is the title?
         Instead of studying at school, red-haired Clarence
     plays with his head lice. He shakes them onto his open
     book, pokes them with a pencil, and slams the book shut
     if the teacher walks by. Name that book!

839. End of a Dark Road by Crystal Thrasher
     Name the book in which Elsworth Starnes puts manure
     in Seely Robinson's only jacket as revenge for her em-
     barrassing him on the school bus.
         Russell Williams has a cruel stepfather named Morton
     Chally. Name the book in which Morton kills Russell's
     mare and her foal, and later, he kills Russell.

840. The Hobbit by J.R.R. Tolkien
     Mr. Bilbo Baggins is a home-loving sort of creature
     who lives quietly in his hole in the ground. In what
     book do thirteen dwarves and a wizard decide to take
     him on an adventure?
         In what book does the Gollum's magic ring save Bilbo
     from certain death, first from the Gollum itself and then
     from the goblins?

841. I, Juan de Pareja by Elizabeth Borton de Trevino
      When Juan's owner dies of the plague, he learns he
      has been inherited, along with the rest of her property,
      by a famous painter. What is this book's title?
      In this book, which takes place in Spain, a slave has
      his ear pierced for a gold earring by his owner. Can
      you give the title?

842. The Adventures of Huckleberry Finn by Mark Twain
      In this book, a boy's father, who is drunk more of-
      ten than sober, threatens his son with a whipping if
      he goes to school again and demands all of his money.
      What is the title?
      This boy stages his own murder with an ax, a pig,
      and a sack of rocks, so no one will follow him when he
      runs away. Name that book!

843. The Adventures of Tom Sawyer by Mark Twain
      Will a dead cat in a graveyard get rid of your warts?
      Tom and his friend never find out but witness a murder
      instead. Name that book!
      When Tom takes the blame for tearing the school-
      master's book, he wins Becky's love forever. Can you
      name this book?

844. The Story of Mankind by Hendrik Van Loon
      Name the history book for children which begins with
      the very first cell of life and takes us up to modern
      times.
      In what children's book will you find a recounting of
      world events, from earliest men to modern days?

845. The Callendar Papers by Cynthia Voigt
      Was Irene Callendar Thiel's death an unfortunate
      accident or was it murder? The answer may be in the
      family's vast collection of papers. This book is called....
      In what book is Jean hired to sort through twelve
      crates of Callendar family papers, looking for the missing
      Callendar will?

846. Dicey's Song by Cynthia Voigt
      Dicey's character sketch about her mentally ill mother
      is so good that her English teacher accuses her of copy-
      ing it from a book. Name her story.
      Dicey and her grandmother don't know how they can

afford to return home from Dicey's mother's funeral until they open the envelope that Maybeth's music teacher gave them. What book are they in?

847. Homecoming by Cynthia Voigt
   Five dollars and fifteen cents, earned by carrying groceries, saves the Tillermans from hunger for a few more days on their long walk to Aunt Cilla's house, in this book called....
   Name the book in which Dicey, James, Maybeth, and Sammy are forced to walk for many, many days to get to their Aunt Cilla's house after their mother abandons them in a mall parking lot.

848. A Solitary Blue by Cynthia Voigt
   When seven-year-old Jeff Green's mother abandons him, she leaves a note that says she loves him very much and that he should fix hot dogs for his father's dinner that night. Name that book!
   Name the book in which Jeff Green always calls his father the Professor and is very careful to never, never upset him.

849. A Chance Child by Jill Paton Walsh
   In what book will you meet Creep, whose mother keeps him locked in a cupboard and who would starve if Christopher didn't sneak him food?
   Lucy wants to marry Tom, but she is so badly scarred that he can hardly stand to look at her. Name that book!

850. The Machine Gunners by Robert Westall
   After a German air-raid on his town in England, Chas McGill discovers a machine gun in the hands of the dead pilot. Name that book!
   A missing machine gun and live ammunition from a downed German plane point the police toward six teen-agers, in this exciting book called....

851. A Little Fear by Patricia Wrightson
   Mrs. Tucker sneaks away from the old folk's home to live in her newly inherited cottage, but there she faces a terrible Njimbin who wants her out! Name that book!
   Strange things happen at Mrs. Tucker's farm. The

dog disappears, the chickens are terrified, and all her
carefully set rat traps are burned. Name the book in
which a creature called a Njimbin is responsible.

852. Dragonwings by Laurence Yep
        Moon Shadow's father believes he was a dragon in
his previous life. Now his greatest goal is to build an
airplane and fly. What is the title of this book?
        To the Tang people, America is the Land of the
Golden Mountain--full of gold and demons. In what
book does eight-year-old Shadow Lee cross the sea to
join his father there?

CHAPTER VII

ADDITIONAL ACTIVITIES
_____

In addition to Battle of Books, NAME THAT BOOK! lends itself to other activities and displays which can help you teach
library skills in novel ways, work with teachers on interdisci-
plinary curriculum units, or simply make the library media
center the most exciting place in school! For example, you
can view the Revolutionary War through the eyes of young
Johnny Tremain, experience the Civil War with teenager Jeff
Bussey in RIFLES FOR WATIE, get acquainted with a mis-
chievious Abe Lincoln in the Aulaires' well-known biography,
spark interest in world geography by having students read
fiction set in various countries, or spice up a nutrition unit
with a generous helping of fiction books featuring food. The
possibilities are limited only by your own imagination.

The following activities are examples of how NAME THAT
BOOK! can be used to incorporate the reading of good fiction
into curricular studies and to stimulate interest in reading.

BULLETIN BOARDS/LEARNING CENTERS

Provide an abundance of pertinent reading material ready for
checkout near the display area. Locate titles by using the
NAME THAT BOOK! index headings at the bottom of each
sample.

1. BOOKS TO MAKE YOU LAUGH

Book questions can be written inside balloon captions
beside a happy clown. After a child has read several of
the books on display and can answer a question correctly,
he/she may write the title and author under the question.

Index heading: "Humor"

2. FICTION U.S.A / READ AROUND THE WORLD

   Display a map of the United States/world surrounded
by book questions on 3" x 5" cards. After reading several books and answering a question correctly, a student
may attach a piece of yarn from the question to the re-
gion of the book's setting.
   Option: Students read nonfiction books and write questions in the style of NAME THAT BOOK!, with the answer
being a state/country. For example, "Which European
country has four official languages?"

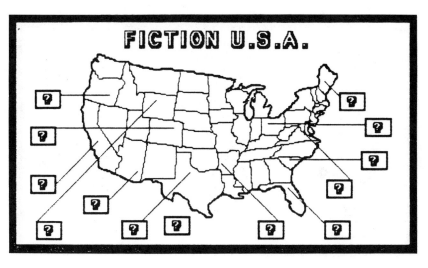

FICTION U.S.A.

   Index headings: "Countries--"; "Folklore--";
   "States--"

3. FOOD FOR THOUGHT

    Use the index of NAME THAT BOOK! to provide a col-
lection of fiction books featuring food, to go along with a
nutrition unit. Book questions can be written on food
shapes for display. After reading the books, students
could list all of the foods presented and have the class
divide them into the four basic food groups, evaluate the
nutritional value of the foods in the stories, or debate
and vote on the best (and worst) diets of the book characters.

Index heading: "Food"

4. GET TO KNOW THE CALDECOTT BOOKS

(GET TO KNOW THE NEWBERY BOOKS)

   Display the Caldecott/Newbery poster of award winners,
obtainable from: Library Binding Service; Treasure Trove
Covers, Box 1413, Des Moines, Iowa 50305. Surround the
poster with book covers of the honor books. Discuss the
meaning of the award and encourage checkout of the books.
Practice questions can be hidden under lift-up replicas
of the medal. Hold a Battle of Caldecott or Newbery
Books.

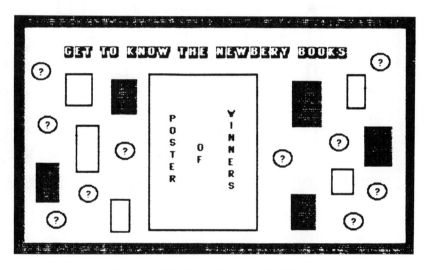

Index headings: "Caldecott Books"; "Newbery Books"

5. HAPPY HOLIDAY READING TO YOU!

  Write questions on brightly colored shapes of paper--
bells for Christmas books, hearts for Valentine's Day books,
turkeys or cornucopias for Thanksgiving books, etc.
Place them on the bulletin board at random and provide
a collection of holiday fiction nearby for checkout. Hold
a Battle of Holiday Books to celebrate each holiday.

Index heading: "Holidays--"

6. SPOOKY BOOKS

A menacing black cat announces October's reading
theme. A Halloween Battle of Books can culminate the
month's activities.

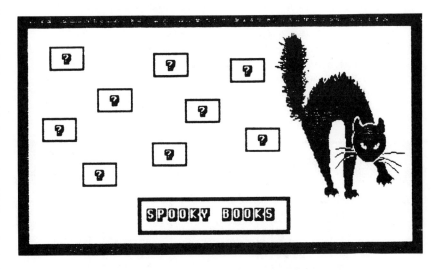

Index headings: "Ghosts"; "Holidays--Halloween";
"Magic"; "Witchcraft"; "Monsters"; "Extrasensory
Perception"

7. MYSTERY AUTHOR

     Here is a bulletin board activity to last the entire
school year! Each week choose an author from the index
of NAME THAT BOOK! who has at least five books listed.
Each day, put up a new question card, beginning with
questions from the author's least known books and pro-
gressing to the better known works. Friday's question
should be from that author's most popular book. Each
student may compete for the weekly prize by completing
one ballot only to guess the author's name. Use the date
and the time of day to decide the winner. See the following page for our sample of a mystery author ballot.

MYSTERY AUTHOR

MONDAY	TUESDAY	WEDNESDAY	THURSDAY	FRIDAY
QUESTION	QUESTION	QUESTION	QUESTION	QUESTION

CAN YOU GUESS THIS AUTHOR?

MYSTERY AUTHOR BALLOT

STUDENT'S NAME:_____

ROOM #_____   DATE:_____

I THINK THE MYSTERY AUTHOR IS:_____
_____

TIME OF DAY:_____

Index headings: "Alexander, Lloyd"; "Blume, Judy";
"Cleary, Beverly"; etc.

8. ON THE TRAIL OF A GOOD MYSTERY

   Intriguing footprints cover questions designed to make
everyone want to read the mysteries on display.

Index heading: "Mystery and Detective"

9. SCHOOL DAZE

Welcome your students back to school in September
with a collection of "school" books and provocative questions about them scattered around a traditional schoolhouse.

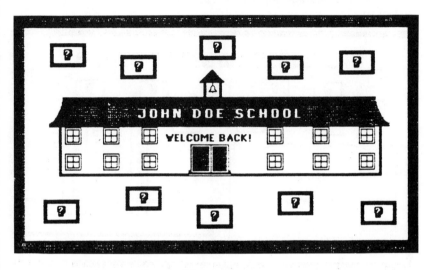

Index heading: "School"

10. SPOTLIGHT ON (AUTHOR)

Display a picture of the featured author (usually obtainable from his/her publisher), book covers, and questions from NAME THAT BOOK! Set up a table of books
by that author for check out.

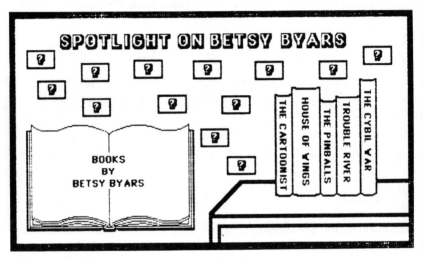

Index headings: same as "Mystery Author"

CURRICULUM UNITS

These suggested study units are designed to overlap several curriculum areas. Ideally, they should involve not only the library media specialist and classroom teacher but also such specialists as counselors, and music and art teachers.

*   *   *

1. AGING (Health/Social Relations/Art) (Gr. 3-6)

(a) Show the series of three free films, "Growing Up, Growing Older," available from Modern Talking Picture Service, 5000 Park Street North, St. Petersburg, Florida 33709. Pre- and post-activities are included.
(b) Display books under an eye-catching collage of people of all ages, constructed by students as an art project.
(c) Provide a file of question cards which children can answer by reading the books on display. Alternately, children can read books at random and write their own questions.
(d) Invite an active retired couple to share their activities with the class.
(e) Arrange a visit to a nursing home. Students may want to become pen pals with some of the residents, or interview them on a tape recorder about their experiences.

Index headings: "Grandparents"; "Old Age"

2. BLACK HISTORY WEEK (Social Studies/Library Skills) (Gr. 6-8)

(a) Concentrate fiction reading on books by and about blacks.
(b) Have students research reference books to make a time line of black history. They could then place a hand-drawn illustration from their fiction book in the appropriate historical period, together with title, author, and setting.
(c) As groupings become obvious, e.g., Pre-Civil War, Depression Era, Present Day, have those students present panel discussions or role-playing on the black experience during that time.

Index headings: "Blacks"; "Slavery"

3. CALDECOTTS (Language Arts/Library Skills/Art) (Gr.
    3-8)

        (a) Display Caldecott winners and honor books.
        (b) Booktalk several; discuss art techniques (colors,
    materials, style).
        (c) Assign students to read and look at a minimum of
    ten books, choosing one for a short report on the illus-
    trator or author/illustrator, as the case may be. Biograph-
    ical sources might be: Junior Book of Authors and Illus-
    trators (H.W. Wilson Co.), The Who's Who of Children's
    Literature (Schocken), Authors and Illustrators of Chil-
    dren's Books by Miriam Hoffman (Bowker), Illustrators of
    Books for Young People by Martha E. Ward (Scarecrow),
    pamphlets from publishers, and book covers.
        (d) Students should illustrate their reports with their
    own picture in the same style as the illustrator, e.g.,
    collage for Keats, woodcut (a potato could substitute) for
    Marcia Brown.
        (e) Another option would be the use of a Visual Maker
    to produce slides for illustrating an oral report.
    (See "Get to Know the Caldecott Books" under BULLE-
    TIN BOARDS/LEARNING CENTERS)

        Index heading: "Caldecott Books"

4. FICTION U.S.A. (Social Studies/Language Arts/Library
    Skills) (Gr. 5-8)

        (a) Along with the usual research on states and cap-
    itals, each student chooses one state from the index of
    NAME THAT BOOK! and reads a fiction book set in that
    locale.
        (b) The student then lists the things he/she learned
    about the state from the fiction book.
        (c) A discussion of setting is a natural beginning to
    discussion of other elements of a story--plot, character-
    ization, style, and theme.
    (See "Fiction U.S.A." under BULLETIN BOARDS/
    LEARNING CENTERS)

        Index headings: "States--"

    ("U.S. History," "Nations at War" and "Countries of
    the World" are also good topics for the incorporation of
    fiction reading into Social Studies units for grades 5-8.)

5. FOLKLORE FOR FUN (Language Arts/Art/Music) (Gr. 3-6)

    (a) Display folktales and books taken from folk songs.
Play records of folk music. Burl Ives' "Froggie Went
a'Courtin'" is ideal.
    (b) The library media specialist can discuss folklore
and booktalk several folktales.
    (c) The music teacher may teach folk songs.
    (d) After studying the components of a folktale and
reading several, assign students to write their own folktale, which may be set to music.

    Index headings: "Folklore--"; "Music"

6. MAKE A READ-ALONG ABOUT INDIANS (Social Studies/
Art/Language Arts/Media Skills) (Gr. 3-5)

    (a) As an enrichment option to classroom study of Na-
tive Americans, set up a diverse collection of easy and
fiction books on Indians in the library media center. Be
sure to include some Indian folklore as well as primary
level reading for slower readers.
    (b) Provide a tape recorder, small bell, blank cassette
tapes, a box for deposit of the students' recorded tapes,
and complete instructions for the student. For example:

    1) Choose one book and read it to yourself.
    2) Insert a blank cassette into the tape recorder.
    3) Push REWIND. When tape is rewound, push STOP.
    4) Push PLAY and RECORD. Make sure they both
       stay down.
    5) Count to three silently, then read the title, the
       author, and your name. For example: "The Girl
       Who Loved Wild Horses by Paul Goble, read by
       John Jones."
    6) Read the book loudly and clearly into the micro-
       phone, ringing the bell for page turns.
When you have finished:
    1) Push STOP.
    2) To listen to your tape, push REWIND, then STOP,
       then PLAY.
    3) Push STOP/EJECT. Remove tape and put in
       "Box for Recorded Tapes."

    (c) Periodically listen to the completed tapes. Label

the best ones with the student's name and the book title
and use them in a listening center.

(d) An appropriate listening center for the read-alongs
would be a big tepee constructed of poles and sheets in
the classroom, media center, or lobby of the school. It
may be decorated with paper bag "buffalo skins" which
the students have decorated with Indian picture writing.

Index headings: "Indians"; "Folklore--Indians"

7. NAME THAT BIOGRAPHY! (Social Studies/Library Skills)
    (Gr. 4-8)

(a) Discuss biographies--definition, location, and ar-
rangement in the library media center.

(b) Have the students read at least one biography.
Instead of reporting on the book, they may be assigned
to write a question on it which will be collected for a game
of "Name That Biography."

(c) Option: Have students act out a scene from the
subject's life for "Biography Charades." This activity
lends itself well to group work.

Index heading: "Biographies"

8. OUT OF THIS WORLD (Science/Language Arts/Art) (Gr.
    6-8)

(a) Display science fiction and fantasy books. Intro-
duce books with a discussion of the definition of these
two related genres.

(b) Have students choose one book to read. They can
then report orally on the elements of fact and fantasy in
their books.

(c) Play a hands-up, no-teams game of Battle of Books
on science fiction and fantasy books. Everyone should be
able to answer at least one question.

(d) An art project could be a model of an imaginary
planet, the solar system, rocket ships, or other means
of space travel. Encourage group work.

Index headings: "Fantasy"; "Science Fiction"; "Space
and Time"

9. RED LETTER DAYS (Language Arts/Library Skills) (Gr.
    K-1)

(a) Display alphabet books in the library media center and/or classroom. Briefly discuss and browse through them with the class.

(b) Name each succeeding day for a letter of the alphabet--"A" Day, "B" Day, etc. Bring as many things as possible to class that begin with that letter.

(c) Show the class the shelf in the Easy book section where they will find books by authors whose last names begin with that letter.

(d) Read one book, watch a filmstrip of a book by a selected author, or booktalk several from that section.

Index heading: "Alphabet Books"

10.   ANIMALS--FACT AND FICTION (Science/Language Arts/ Library Skills/Art) (Gr. 2-5)

(a) Discuss with students the difference between fiction and nonfiction books. Show where each is located in the library media center. Show the specific location and number of the nonfiction books on animals.

(b) Have students choose one animal (you may want them to begin with mammals as a first assignment) from the index of NAME THAT BOOK! They are to read one nonfiction and one fiction book about that animal.

(c) They may write a short factual report from the nonfiction book, as well as tell "the best part" from their fiction book. Be sure to discuss the differences they found between the two books.

(d) Students may make papier mâché replicas of their animals as an art project.

(e) As a promotion for the unit, have the children bring stuffed animals from home. Label each and set up as a super display in the library media center. A wildlife officer may also be invited to bring animals and give a talk.

Index headings: "Animals--"

FUN AND GAMES

1.   BACKWARD BATTLE OF BOOKS

Name an author. Students raise hands to name as

many of that author's works as they can. The student
who gives the last title gets to name another author.

2. BASEBALL BY THE BOOK

Divide the class into two teams. Arrange chairs for
first, second, third base, and home plate.
The pitcher addresses questions to individuals "up to
bat."
A correct title moves the batter to first base; correct
title and author constitutes a home run.
The runner may steal bases by raising his/her hand
to give a correct answer if the batter misses the question.
Since only one runner may occupy a base at a time, run-
ners may also be "batted in" by their team mates.
If a batter cannot answer the question correctly, he/
she has one strike. However, if none of the opposing
team members can answer the same question, the batter
receives two balls.
Three strikes constitute an out, four balls walk the
batter to first base. Three outs retire the side and the
other team comes up to bat.

3. BOOK BEE

"Book Bee" is played exactly like a spelling bee except
that instead of words to spell, students are given book
questions to answer. The last student left standing is
the Queen (or King) Bee.

4. BOOK CHARADES

Divide the class into teams of three to four people.
Write the titles and authors of popular books on slips of
paper and have each team draw one from a hat. Give the
teams five to ten minutes to prepare their skits, which
may be a scene from the book or an acting out of the
actual title of the book. The rest of the class tries to
guess the title and author as the skits are presented.

5. CARD CATALOG FUN AND PRACTICE--AUTHOR AND
    TITLE CARDS

Write out book questions on index cards, leaving a
blank for names of places or characters. Include title of

the book but not author, or vice versa. Each team or individual earns one point for locating the book on the shelf and two points for filling in the blank correctly.

6. CARD CATALOG FUN AND PRACTICE--SUBJECT CARDS

Give each individual or team of students a different subject. They must write down the title, author, and call number of a nonfiction and a fiction book on that subject. Give extra points for locating both books on the shelf. Consult the index of NAME THAT BOOK! and your card catalog for subjects.

7. GO AND GET IT BATTLE OF BOOKS

Divide the class into two teams for Battle of Books. When a correct title and author have been given by one team, let the other team have first chance to earn four more points by locating the book on the shelf within 60 seconds.

8. THE LINE-UP (For the last five minutes before the bell rings when there is no time to begin an involved activity.)

Ask rapid-fire book questions to individual students. If a correct response is given, the student takes his/her place in line. Students missing the question remain seated until you come around to them again. Of course, direct easiest questions to slow/reluctant readers.

9. SUBJECT BATTLE OF BOOKS

Name a subject, for example, "Horses." Students try to name a fiction book about that subject. After a title has been given, students try to name the author. Consult the index of NAME THAT BOOK! for subjects.

10. TURN ABOUT

Battle of Books questions are directed to the class. Members raise hands to answer. The student giving the correct response gets to ask the questions until another correct response is given.

AUTHOR INDEX

(Numbers in brackets indicate the number of books by author on designated page)

TITLE INDEX

(Animals, cont'd.)

    Bemelmans, Ludwig. Madeline's Rescue 20
    Bonsall, Crosby. And I Mean It, Stanley 8
    Branscum, Robbie. Murder of Hound Dog Bates, The 69
    Bridwell, Norman. Clifford the Big Red Dog 9
    Burnford, Sheila. Incredible Journey, The 83
    Carrick, Carol. Accident, The 22
    Cleary, Beverly. Henry Huggins 48
    Cohen, Peter Zachary. Deadly Game at Stony Creek 103
    Cone, Molly. MishMash 59
    Corbett, Scott. Disappearing Dog Trick, The 59
    DeJong, Meindert. Along Came a Dog 87; Hurry Home,
       Candy 87
    Estes, Eleanor. Ginger Pye 88
    Gardiner, John Reynolds. Stone Fox 61
    Gipson, Fred. Old Yeller 122; Savage Sam 107
    Girion, Barbara. Misty and Me 72
    Gray, Elizabeth Janet. Adam of the Road 153
    Hoff, Syd. Barkley 13
    Howe, Deborah and James. Bunnicula; A Rabbit Tale of
       Mystery 62
    Howe, James. Howliday Inn 62
    Kjelgaard, Jim. Big Red 93
    Knight, Eric. Lassie Come-Home 124
    Lipkind, William and Nicholas Mordvinof. Finders Keepers
       15
    London, Jack. Call of the Wild, The 158
    McInerney, Judith Whitelock. Judge Benjamin: Superdog
       74
    Rawls, Wilson. Where the Red Fern Grows 144
    Shura, Mary Francis. Mr. Wolf and Me 77
    Smith, Doris Buchanan. Moonshadow of Cherry Mountain
       130
    Stevens, Carla. Trouble for Lucy 65
    Van Allsburg, Chris. Garden of Abdul Gasazi, The 44
    Wallace, Bill. Dog Called Kitty, A 98
    Zion, Gene. Harry the Dirty Dog 18
--Dolphins
    L'Engle, Madeleine. Ring of Endless Light, A 142
--Donkeys
    Steig, William. Sylvester and the Magic Pebble 42
--Dragons
    Hodges, Margaret. Saint George and the Dragon 51
    Sargent, Sarah. Weird Henry Berg 113
    Yep, Laurence. Dragon of the Lost Sea 132
--Elephants
    Brunhoff, Jean De. Story of Babar, The 21
    Kipling, Rudyard. Elephant's Child, The 33
    Seuss, Dr. Horton Hatches the Egg 40
--Ferrets
    Dana, Barbara. Zucchini 86

(Animals, cont'd.)
--Fish
    Cleary, Beverly. <u>Henry Huggins</u> 48
    Cohen, Barbara. <u>Carp in the Bathtub, The</u> 23
    Seuss, Dr. <u>McElligot's Pool</u> 41
    Yorinks, Arthur. <u>Louis the Fish</u> 18
--Forest animals
    George, Jean Craighead. <u>My Side of the Mountain</u> 122
    Hader, Berta and Elmer. <u>Big Snow, The</u> 29
--Foxes
    Chaucer, Geoffrey. <u>Chanticleer and the Fox</u> 23
--Frogs and Toads
    Erickson, Russell. <u>Toad for Tuesday</u> 50; <u>Warton and the</u>
       <u>Traders</u> 50
    Lobel, Arnold. <u>Frog and Toad Are Friends</u> 15; <u>Frog and</u>
       <u>Toad Together</u> 15
--Goats
    Sharmat, Mitchell. <u>Gregory the Terrible Eater</u> 17
--Hippopotami
    Marshall, James. <u>George and Martha</u> 35
--Horses
    Anderson, C. W. <u>Billy and Blaze</u> 7
    Doty, Jean Slaughter. <u>Valley of the Ponies</u> 60
    Dunn, Marylois. <u>Absolutely Perfect Horse, The</u> 121
    Goble, Paul. <u>Gift of the Sacred Dog, The</u> 28; <u>Girl Who</u>
       <u>Loved Wild Horses, The</u> 28
    Hall, Lynn. <u>Danza</u> 123
    Henry, Marguerite. <u>Justin Morgan Had a Horse</u> 91; <u>King</u>
       <u>of the Wind</u> 91; <u>Misty of Chincoteague</u> 91
    James, Will. <u>Smoky, the Cowhorse</u> 141
    Morey, Walt. <u>Year of the Black Pony</u> 110
    Otsuka, Yuzo. <u>Suho and the White Horse</u> 37
    Rounds, Glen. <u>Blind Outlaw</u> 76
    Sandoz, Mari. <u>Horsecatcher, The</u> 145
--Insects
    Carle, Eric. <u>Very Hungry Caterpillar, The</u> 10
    Hass, E. A. <u>Incognito Mosquito, Private Insective</u> 62
    Kherdian, David. <u>Song in the Walnut Grove, The</u> 92
    Lord, John. <u>Giant Jam Sandwich, The</u> 35
    Selden, George. <u>Chester Cricket's New Home</u> 76; <u>Cricket</u>
       <u>in Times Square, The</u> 76; <u>Harry Cat's Pet Puppy</u> 77
--Jungle animals
    Aardema, Verna. <u>Who's in Rabbit's House?</u> 18; <u>Why Mos-</u>
       <u>quitos Buzz in People's Ears</u> 18
    Kipling, Rudyard. <u>Jungle Book, The</u> 93
--Lions
    Aesop. <u>Lion and the Mouse, The</u> 6
    Daugherty, James. <u>Andy and the Lion</u> 10
    Fatio, Louise. <u>Happy Lion, The</u> 26
--Lizards
    Massie, Diane. <u>Chameleon Was a Spy</u> 35

(Animals, cont'd.)
  --Llamas
      Clark, Ann Nolan. Secret of the Andes 137
  --Mice
      Aesop. Lion and the Mouse, The 6
      Brown, Marcia. Once a Mouse 21
      Cleary, Beverly. Mouse and the Motorcycle, The 57; Ralph
        S. Mouse 57; Runaway Ralph 58
      Drury, Roger W. Champion of Merrimack County, The 87
      Flack, Marjorie. Walter the Lazy Mouse 27
      Kellogg, Steven. Island of the Skog, The 32
      Kraus, Robert. Whose Mouse Are You? 14
      Lionni, Leo. Alexander and the Wind-Up Mouse 34; Fred-
        erick 34
      O'Brien, Robert C. Mrs. Frisby and the Rats of NIMH 126
      Selden, George. Cricket in Times Square 76; Harry Cat's
        Pet Puppy 77
      Steig, William. Abel's Island 78; Dr. De Soto 42
      Titus, Eve. Anatole 43
      Van Leeuwen, Jean. Great Christmas Kidnapping Caper, The
        79; Great Rescue Operation, The 79
  --Monkeys
      Hoban, Lillian. Arthur's Honey Bear 13
      Rawls, Wilson. Summer of the Monkeys 144
      Rey, H. A. Curious George 16
      Slobodkina, Esphyr. Caps for Sale 17
  --Otters
      Benchley, Nathaniel. Oscar Otter 8
      Hoban, Russell. Emmet Otter's Jug-Band Christmas 30
  --Pigs
      Callen, Larry. Pinch 103
      Marshall, James. Yummers! 35
      Rayner, Mary. Mrs. Pig's Bulk Buy 39
      Steig, William. Amazing Bone, The 42
      White, E. B. Charlotte's Web 80
  --Possums
      Conford, Ellen. Impossible Possum 23
  --Rabbits
      Adams, Adrienne. Great Valentine's Day Balloon Race, The
        19
      Adams, Richard. Watership Down 147
      Brown, Margaret Wise. Runaway Bunny, The 9
      DeJong, Meindert. Shadrach 87
      Heyward, Du Bose. Country Bunny and the Little Gold
        Shoes, The 30
      Howe, Deborah and James. Bunnicula; A Rabbit Tale of
        Mystery 62
      Lawson, Robert. Rabbit Hill 74
      Newberry, Clare. Marshmallow 37
      Potter, Beatrix. Tale of Peter Rabbit, The 38
      Zolotow, Charlotte. Mr. Rabbit and the Lovely Present 18

(Animals, cont'd.)
--Raccoons
    North, Sterling. Rascal 143
--Seals
    Hunter, Mollie. Stranger Came Ashore, A 141
--Snakes
    Noble, Trinka Hakes. Day Jimmy's Boa Ate the Wash, The
    37
--Spiders
    Graham, Margaret. Be Nice to Spiders 12
    White, E. B. Charlotte's Web 80
--Squirrels
    Zion, Gene. Meanest Squirrel I Ever Met, The 45
--Wolves
    Aiken, Joan. Wolves of Willoughby Chase, The 100
    George, Jean Craighead. Julie of the Wolves 139
    Stewart, Mary. Walk in Wolf Wood, A 131
--Worms
    Lionni, Leo. Inch by Inch 34

BIOGRAPHIES/AUTOBIOGRAPHIES
    Coerr, Eleanor. Sadako and the Thousand Paper Cranes
    71
    D'Aulaire, Ingri and Edgar. Abraham Lincoln 24
    Fritz, Jean. George Washington's Breakfast 27; Homesick:
    My Own Story 122
    Latham, Jean Lee. Carry On, Mr. Bowditch 157
    Lawson, Robert. They Were Strong and Good 33
    Meigs, Cornelia. Invincible Louisa 143
    Reiss, Johanna. Upstairs Room, The 161
    Yates, Elizabeth. Amos Fortune, Free Man 132

BLACKS
    Adoff, Arnold. Black Is Brown Is Tan 19
    Armstrong, William. Sounder 116
    Brooks, Bruce. Moves Make the Man, The 149
    Childress, Alice. Hero Ain't Nothing but a Sandwich, A
    149
    Collier, James Lincoln and Christopher. War Comes to Willy
    Freeman 150
    Fenner, Carol. Skates of Uncle Richard, The 60
    Fox, Paula. How Many Miles to Babylon? 122
    Greene, Bette. Get On Out of Here, Philip Hall 123; Philip
    Hall Likes Me, I Reckon Maybe 89
    Hamilton, Virginia. House of Dies Drear, The 153; M. C.
    Higgins, the Great 153; Willie Bea and the Time the Mar-
    tians Landed 154
    Hooks, William H. Circle of Fire 107
    Hurmence, Belinda. Girl Called Boy, A 141; Tancy 155;
    Tough Tiffany 141
    Lexau, Joan. Striped Ice Cream 63

(Blacks, cont'd.)
      Mathis, Sharon Bell. Hundred Penny Box, The 64
      Merrill, Jean. Toothpaste Millionaire, The 94
      Moore, Emily. Something to Count On 94
      Neufeld, John. Edgar Allan 111
      Steptoe, John. Daddy Is a Monster ... Sometimes 42
      Tate, Eleanora E. Just an Overnight Guest 131
      Taylor, Mildred. Roll of Thunder, Hear My Cry 145; Song
            of the Trees 66
      Weik, Mary H. Jazz Man, The 54
      Yates, Elizabeth. Amos Fortune, Free Man 132

BROTHERS AND SISTERS
      Adler, Carole S. Get Lost, Little Brother 80
      Alcott, Louisa May. Little Women 147
      Alexander, Martha. Nobody Asked Me If I Wanted a Baby
            Sister 6
      Blume, Judy. One in the Middle Is the Green Kangaroo, The
            21; Superfudge 55; Tales of a Fourth Grade Nothing 55
      Bonsall, Crosby. Who's a Pest? 9
      Byars, Betsy . Animal, the Vegetable, and John D. Jones,
            The 102; Go and Hush the Baby 22; Night Swimmers
            The 102; Summer of the Swans, The 103
      Cleary, Beverly. Mitch and Amy 48
      Cleaver, Vera and Bill. Where the Lilies Bloom 149
      Clifford, Eth. Help! I'm a Prisoner in the Library 58
      Clymer, Eleanor. My Brother Stevie 70
      Fitzgerald, John D. Great Brain, The 105
      Giff, Patricia Reilly. Gift of the Pirate Queen, The 89
      Greene, Constance C. Beat the Turtle Drum 123; I and
            Sproggy 89
      Greenwald, Sheila. Give Us a Great Big Smile, Rosie Cole
            51
      Hermes, Patricia. Who Will Take Care of Me? 107
      Hinton, S. E. Outsiders, The 154; Tex 154
      Hoban, Lillian. Arthur's Honey Bear 13
      Hughes, Shirley. David and Dog 31; George the Babysitter
            31
      Isadora, Rachel. Max 32
      Keats, Ezra Jack. Peter's Chair 14
      Lowry, Lois. Summer to Die, A 109
      McCord, Jean. Turkeylegs Thompson 143
      Moeri, Louise. Save Queen of Sheba 109
      Naylor, Phyllis. Solomon System, The 111
      Oppenheimer, Joan L. Gardine vs. Hanover 126
      Park, Barbara. Operation: Dump the Chump 64
      Paterson, Katherine. Jacob Have I Loved 160
      Peck, Richard. Don't Look and It Won't Hurt 161
      Pevsner, Stella. And You Give Me a Pain, Elaine 144
      Shyer, Marlene Fanta. My Brother the Thief 129; Welcome
            Home, Jellybean 130

(Countries, cont'd.)
  --Switzerland
      Spyri, Johanna. Heidi 145
  --Turkey
      Kherdian, David. Road from Home: The Story of an Armen-
        ian Girl, The 156

DEATH
      Bawden, Nina. Squib 117
      Carner, Chas. Tawny 149
      Carrick, Carol. Accident, The 22
      Cleaver, Vera and Bill. Grover 85; Where the Lilies Bloom
        149
      Coerr, Eleanor. Sadako and the Thousand Paper Cranes
        71
      Graeber, Charlotte. Mustard 50
      Greene, Constance C. Beat the Turtle Drum 123
      Hughes, Dean. Switching Tracks 140
      Langton, Jane. Fledgling, The 73
      L'Engle, Madeleine. Ring of Endless Light, A 142
      Lowry, Lois. Summer to Die, A 109
      Mann, Peggy. There Are Two Kinds of Terrible 125
      Miles, Miska. Annie and the Old One 53
      Ness, Evaline. Sam, Bangs and Moonshine 37
      Paterson, Katherine. Bridge to Terabithia 95
      Smith, Doris Buchanan. Taste of Blackberries, A 78
      Strete, Craig. When Grandfather Journeys into Winter 78
      Taha, Karen. Gift for Tia Rosa, A 43
      White, E. B. Charlotte's Web 80
      York, Carol Beach. Remember Me When I Am Dead 132

DIVORCE
      Blue, Rose. Month of Sundays, A 55
      Blume, Judy. It's Not the End of the World 101
      Cleary, Beverly. Dear Mr. Henshaw 57
      Gerson, Corinne. How I Put My Mother Through College
        106
      Greene, Constance C. Ask Anybody 89
      Mann, Peggy. My Dad Lives in a Downtown Hotel 63
      Mazer, Norma Fox. Taking Terri Mueller 158
      McCord, Jean. Turkeylegs Thompson 143
      Moore, Emily. Something to Count On 94
      Naylor, Phyllis. Solomon System, The 111
      Voigt, Cynthia. Solitary Blue, A 165

EXTRASENSORY PERCEPTION
      Peck, Richard. Ghost Belonged to Me, The 127; Ghosts I
        Have Been 127
      Phipson, Jean. Watcher in the Garden, The 161
      Roberts, Willo Davis. Girl With Silver Eyes, The 128
      Rodowsky, Colby. Evy-Ivy-Over 129

(Extrasensory Perception, cont'd.)
    Sleator, William. Into the Dream 96
    Wright, Betty Ren. Secret Window, The 115

FAMILY LIFE
    Adoff, Arnold. Black Is Brown Is Tan 19
    Blaine, Marge. Terrible Thing That Happened at Our House,
      The 20
    Blume, Judy. Superfudge 55; Tales of a Fourth Grade
      Nothing 55; Then Again, Maybe I Won't 101
    Byars, Betsy. Cartoonist, The 83; Glory Girl, The 84
    Cameron, Eleanor. That Julia Redfern 70
    Cleary, Beverly. Mitch and Amy 48; Ramona and Her Father
      58; Ramona and Her Mother 58; Ramona Forever 48; Ra-
      mona Quimby, Age 8 48; Ramona the Brave 49; Socks
      58
    Cleaver, Vera and Bill. Ellen Grae 84; Hazel Rye 137;
      Queen of Hearts 137
    Clymer, Eleanor. My Mother Is the Smartest Woman in the
      World 49
    Conford, Ellen. Luck of Pokey Bloom, The 104
    Danziger, Paula. Pistachio Prescription, The 104
    Estes, Eleanor. Ginger Pye 88
    Fenner, Carol. Skates of Uncle Richard, The 60
    Gilson, Jamie. Can't Catch Me, I'm the Gingerbread Man
      71
    Girion, Barbara. Misty and Me 72
    Greene, Constance C. Al(exandra) the Great 89
    Greenwald, Sheila. All the Way to Wit's End 90; Will the
      Real Gertrude Hollings Please Stand Up? 123
    Hazen, Barbara Shook. Tight Times 30
    Hill, Elizabeth. Evan's Corner 30
    Holland, Isabelle. Dinah and the Green Fat Kingdom 124
    Hurmence, Belinda. Tough Tiffany 141
    Hurwitz, Johanna. Aldo Ice Cream 62; Baseball Fever 63;
      Much Ado About Aldo 52; Rabbi's Girls, The 72; Rip-
      Roaring Russell 52; Tough Luck Karen 92
    Kerr, M. E. Dinky Hocker Shoots Smack! 156
    Kibbe, Pat. Hocus-Pocus Dilemma 73
    Lexau, Joan. Striped Ice Cream 63
    MacLachlan, Patricia. Arthur for the Very First Time 109;
      Seven Kisses in a Row 52
    Mann, Peggy. There Are Two Kinds of Terrible 125
    McInerney, Judith Whitelock. Judge Benjamin: Superdog
      74
    O'Connor, Jane. Just Good Friends 143
    Park, Ruth. Playing Beatie Bow 160
    Pearce, Phillipa. Way to Satin Shore, The 126
    Pellowski, Anne. Betsy's Up-and-Down Year 75; Willow
      Wind Farm: Betsy's Story 75
    Pevsner, Stella. And You Give Me a Pain, Elaine 144

(Folklore, cont'd.)
        De Paola, Tomie. Clown of God, The 24
    --Great Britain
        Galdone, Paul. King of the Cats 28
        Hodges, Margaret. Saint George and the Dragon 51
        Hunter, Mollie. Stranger Came Ashore, A 141
        Minard, Rosemary. Long Meg 53
        Zemach, Harve. Duffy and the Devil: A Cornish Tale 45
    --Hungary
        Seredy, Kate. White Stag, The 113
    --India
        Brown, Marcia. Once a Mouse 21
    --Indian (American)
        Baker, Olaf. Where the Buffaloes Begin 68
        De Paola, Tomie. Legend of the Bluebonnet; An Old Tale
            of Texas, The 24
        Finger, Charles J. Tales from Silver Lands 122
        Highwater, Jamake. Anpao: An American Indian Odyssey
            154
        McDermott, Gerald. Arrow to the Sun; A Pueblo Indian Tale
            36
        Sleator, William. Angry Moon, The 42
    --Italy
        De Paola, Tomie. Strega Nona: An Old Tale Retold 25
    --Mongolia
        Otsuka, Yuzo. Suho and the White Horse 37
    --Russia
        Ransome, Arthur. Fool of the World and the Flying Ship,
            The 39
        Reyher, Becky. My Mother Is the Most Beautiful Woman in
            the World 39
        Robbins, Ruth. Baboushka and the Three Kings 39

FOOD
        Asch, Frank. Popcorn 7
        Babbitt, Natalie. Search for Delicious, The 81
        Berenstain, Stanley and Janice. Big Honey Hunt, The 8
        Brown, Marcia. Stone Soup 21
        Catling, Patrick. Chocolate Touch, The 57
        Dahl, Roald. Charlie and the Chocolate Factory 86; James
            and the Giant Peach 86
        Devlin, Wende and Harry. Cranberry Thanksgiving 26
        Fritz, Jean. George Washington's Breakfast 27
        Gilson, Jamie. Can't Catch Me, I'm the Gingerbread Man
            71
        Heide, Florence Parry. Banana Blitz 90; Banana Twist 91
        Howe, Deborah and James. Bunnicula; A Rabbit Tale of Mys-
            tery 62
        Hurwitz, Johanna. Tough Luck Karen 92
        Kellogg, Steven. Ralph's Secret Weapon 33
        Kent, Jack. Fat Cat 33

GHOSTS

HOLIDAYS

--Christmas

--Easter

--Halloween

--New Year's Day

--Thanksgiving

--Valentine's Day

HUMOR

Allard, Harry. Stupids Have a Ball, The 7
Atwater, Richard and Florence. Mr. Popper's Penguins 68
Barrett, Judi. Animals Should Definitely NOT Wear Clothing
    8
Beatty, Patricia. That's One Ornery Orphan 101
Berenstain, Stanley and Janice. Big Honey Hunt, The 8
Bethancourt, T. Ernesto. T.H.U.M.B. 136
Blume, Judy. Freckle Juice 47; One in the Middle Is the
    Green Kangaroo, The 21; Superfudge 55; Tales of a
    Fourth Grade Nothing 55
Bottner, Barbara. Dumb Old Casey Is a Fat Tree 47
Brittain, Bill. All the Money in the World 69
Burch, Robert. Christmas with Ida Early 82; Ida Early
    Comes over the Mountain 83
Byars, Betsy. Eighteenth Emergency, The 56; TV Kid, The
    70
Callen, Larry. Pinch 103
Catling, Patrick. Chocolate Touch, The 57
Cleary, Beverly. Ellen Tebbits 48; Henry Huggins 48;
    Mouse and the Motorcycle, The 57; Otis Spofford 57;
    Ramona and Her Father 58; Ramona and Her Mother 58;
    Ramona Forever 48; Ramona Quimby, Age 8 48; Ramona
    the Brave 49; Runaway Ralph 58; Socks 58
Cone, Molly. MishMash 59
Conford, Ellen. Anything for a Friend 119; Felicia the
    Critic 85; Lenny Kandell, Smart Aleck 103; Luck of
    Pokey Bloom, The 104; Me and the Terrible Two 59
Cusack, Isabel Langis. Ivan the Great 49
Dahl, Roald. B.F.G., The 85; Charlie and the Chocolate
    Factory 86; Charlie and the Great Glass Elevator 86;
    Danny, the Champion of the World 86
Danziger, Paula. There's a Bat in Bunk Five 104
De Paola, Tomie. Strega Nona: An Old Tale Retold 25
Drury, Roger W. Champion of Merrimack County, The 87
Fitzgerald, John D. Great Brain, The 105
Fitzhugh, Louise. Harriet the Spy 105
Fleischman, Paul. Finzel the Farsighted 50
Fleischman, Sid. Ghost on Saturday Night, The 61; Hum-
    bug Mountain 106; McBroom and the Beanstalk 50;
    McBroom Tells a Lie 50
Gackenbach, Dick. Harry and the Terrible Whatzit 12
Giff, Patricia Reilly. Fourth Grade Celebrity 61; Left-
    Handed Shortstop 61
Gilson, Jamie. 4B Goes Wild 61; Can't Catch Me, I'm the
    Gingerbread Man 71; Do Bananas Chew Gum? 106;
    Harvey, the Beer Can King 71; Thirteen Ways to Sink
    a Sub 62
Green, Phyllis. Eating Ice Cream with a Werewolf 51
Greene, Bette. Philip Hall Likes Me, I Reckon Maybe 89
Greene, Constance C. Al(exandra) the Great 89

(Humor, cont'd.)
  Rockwell, Thomas. How to Eat Fried Worms 76
  Rodgers, Mary. Freaky Friday 112; Summer Switch 112
  Rounds, Glen. Mr. Yowder and the Train Robbers 53;
    Mr. Yowder and the Windwagon 54
  Salassi, Otto. On the Ropes 161
  Sawyer, Ruth. Roller Skates 129
  Sharmat, Marjorie. Mysteriously Yours, Maggie Marmelstein
    77; Getting Something on Maggie Marmelstein 77
  Simon, Seymour. Einstein Anderson Makes Up for Lost Time
    77
  Smith, Allison. Help! There's a Cat Washing in Here 96
  Travers, P. L. Mary Poppins 79
  Twain, Mark. Adventures of Tom Sawyer, The 164
  Wallace, Barbara Brooks. Hawkins 79; Hawkins and the
    Soccer Solution 79
  Wilkes, Marilyn Z. C.L.U.T.Z. 99
  Williams, Barbara. Mitzi and the Terrible Tyrannosaurus Rex
    67
  Wolkoff, Judie. Happily Ever After--Almost 115

INDIANS [AMERICAN]
  Armer, Laura Adams Waterless Mountain 148
  Baker, Olaf. Where the Buffaloes Begin 68
  Banks, Lynne Reid. Indian in the Cupboard, The 100
  Baylor, Byrd. Hawk, I'm Your Brother 20
  Byars, Betsy. Trouble River 69
  Clark, Ann Nolan. Secret of the Andes 137
  Dalgliesh, Alice. Courage of Sarah Noble, The 60
  De Paola, Tomie. Legend of the Bluebonnet; An Old Tale
    of Texas, The 24
  Edmonds, Walter. Matchlock Gun, The 71
  Finger, Charles J. Tales from Silver Lands 122
  George, Jean Craighead. Talking Earth, The 152
  Gipson, Fred. Savage Sam 107
  Goble, Paul. Gift of the Sacred Dog, The 28; Girl Who
    Loved Wild Horses, The 28
  Highwater, Jamake. Anpao: An American Indian Odyssey
    154; Moonsong Lullaby 30
  McDermott, Gerald. Arrow to the Sun; A Pueblo Indian Tale
    36
  Miles, Miska. Annie and the Old One 53
  O'Dell, Scott. Island of the Blue Dolphins 126; Sing Down
    the Moon 126; Zia 160
  Sandoz, Mari. Horsecatcher, The 145
  Sleator, William. Angry Moon, The 42
  Speare, Elizabeth. Sign of the Beaver, The 145
  Strete, Craig. When Grandfather Journeys into Winter 78

MAGIC
  Banks, Lynne Reid. Indian in the Cupboard, The 100

(Magic, cont'd.)
>
Bellairs, John. Curse of the Blue Figurine, The 117; Figure
  in the Shadows, The 118; House with a Clock in Its Walls,
  The 118; Mummy, the Will, and the Crypt, The 118
Brittain, Bill. All the Money in the World 69; Devil's Don-
  key 56; Wish Giver: Three Tales of Coven Tree, The
  69
Chew, Ruth. Earthstar Magic 57
Corbett, Scott. Baseball Trick, The 59; Disappearing Dog
  Trick, The 59; Lemonade Trick, The 60
Dahl, Roald. James and the Giant Peach 86; Magic Finger,
  The 49
De Paola, Tomie. Big Anthony and the Magic Ring 24;
  Helga's Dowry: A Troll Love Story 24; Strega Nona's
  Magic Lessons 25; Strega Nona: An Old Tale Retold 25
Devlin, Wende. Old Black Witch 25
Fleming, Ian. Chitty-Chitty-Bang-Bang 88
Kibbe, Pat. Hocus-Pocus Dilemma 73
Lewis, C. S. Last Battle, The 108
MacDonald, Betty. Mrs. Piggle Wiggle 63
Mahy, Margaret. Haunting, The 158
McGraw, Eloise Jarvis. Joel and the Great Merlini 74
Mosel, Arlene. Funny Little Woman, The 36
Steig, William. Amazing Bone, The 42; Sylvester and the
  Magic Pebble 42
Travers, P. L. Mary Poppins 79
Van Allsburg, Chris. Garden of Abdul Gasazi, The 44
Wrightson, Patricia. Little Fear, A 165

MONSTERS
>
Bang, Molly. Wiley and the Hairy Man 19
Calhoun, Mary. Night the Monster Came, The 56
Crowe, Robert L. Clyde Monster 24
Gackenbach, Dick. Harry and the Terrible Whatzit 12
Green, Phyllis. Eating Ice Cream with a Werewolf 51
Kellogg, Steven. Island of the Skog, The 32; Mysterious
  Tadpole, The 32
Mayer, Mercer. There's a Nightmare in My Closet 15
Pinkwater, Daniel Manus. I Was a Second-Grade Werewolf
  38; Yobgorgle: Mystery Monster of Lake Ontario 111
Sendak, Maurice. Where the Wild Things Are 16

MUSIC
>
Bethancourt, T. Ernesto. T.H.U.M.B. 136
Emberly, Barbara. One Wide River to Cross 11
Greene, Bette. Them That Glitter and Them That Don't
  139
Hentoff, Nat. Does This School Have Capital Punishment?
  139
Hoban, Russell. Emmet Otter's Jug-Band Christmas 30
Hopper, Nancy J. Hang On, Harvey! 107

(Music, cont'd.)
    Hurd, Thacher. Mystery on the Docks 31
    Isadora, Rachel. Ben's Trumpet 31
    Kidd, Ronald. Sizzle and Splat 124
    Langstaff, John. Frog Went A-Courtin' 14
    Leodhas, Sorche Nic. Always Room for One More 34
    Morey, Walter. Sandy and the Rock Star 110
    Prokokiev, Sergei. Peter and the Wolf 16
    Seidler, Tor. Dulcimer Boy, The 113
    Sleator, William. Fingers 162
    Walter, Mildred Pitts. Ty's One-Man Band 54

MYSTERY AND DETECTIVE
    Babbitt, Natalie. Knee-Knock Rise 68
    Bawden, Nina. Squib 117
    Bellairs, John. Curse of the Blue Figurine, The 117; Figure in the Shadows, The 118; House with a Clock in Its Walls, The 118; Mummy, the Will, and the Crypt, The 118
    Branscum, Robbie. Murder of Hound Dog Bates, The 69
    Brookins, Dana. Alone in Wolf Hollow 102
    Cameron, Eleanor. Court of the Stone Children, The 136
    Clyne, Patricia Edwards. Curse of Camp Gray Owl, The 85
    Corcoran, Barbara. Person in the Potting Shed, The 120
    Curry, Jane Louise. Ghost Lane 120
    Elmore, Patricia. Susannah and the Blue House Mystery 87
    Erwin, Betty K. Go to the Room of the Eyes 105
    Fleischman, Paul. Phoebe Danger, Detective, in the Case of the Two-Minute Cough 61
    Hamilton, Virginia. House of Dies Drear, The 153
    Hass, E. A. Incognito Mosquito, Private Insective 62
    Hicks, Clifford. Alvin's Swap Shop 92
    Holland, Isabelle. Empty House, The 155
    Howe, James. Howliday Inn 62
    Hurd, Thacher. Mystery on the Docks 31
    Hutchins, Pat. Mona Lisa Mystery, The 52
    Kidd, Ronald. Sizzle and Splat 124
    Klaveness, Jan O'Donnell. Griffin Legacy, The 157
    Lowry, Lois. One Hundredth Thing About Caroline, The 94
    McGraw, Eloise Jarvis. Money Room, The 109
    McHargue, Georgess. Turquoise Toad Mystery, The 109
    Newman, Robert. Case of the Baker Street Irregular, The 159
    Pearce, Phillipa. Way to Satin Shore, The 126
    Raskin, Ellen. Westing Game, The 128
    Roberts, Willo Davis. Pet-Sitting Peril, The 128
    Sobol, Donald. Angie's First Case 97
    Voigt, Cynthia. Callender Papers, The 164
    Wallace, Barbara Brooks. Peppermints in the Parlor 114

NEWBERY BOOKS

SURVIVAL
    Burnford, Sheila. Incredible Journey, The   83
    Chambers, John W. Fritzi's Winter   84
    Clifford, Eth. Curse of the Moonraker, The   150
    Defoe, Daniel. Robinson Crusoe   151
    Eckert, Allan W. Incident at Hawk's Hill   152
    George, Jean Craighead. Julie of the Wolves   139; My Side
       of the Mountain   122; Talking Earth, The   152
    Holman, Felice. Slake's Limbo   140; Wild Children, The   140
    Houston, James. Frozen Fire; A Tale of Courage   140; Long
       Claws; An Arctic Adventure   72
    Lawrence, Louise. Calling B for Butterfly   93
    London, Jack. Call of the Wild, The   158
    Moeri, Louise. Save Queen of Sheba   109
    O'Brien, Robert C. Z for Zachariah   159
    O'Dell, Scott. Island of the Blue Dolphins   126
    Petersen, P. J. Nobody Else Can Walk It for You   161
    Skurzynski, Gloria. Caught in the Moving Mountains   96;
       Lost in the Devil's Desert   113
    Sperry, Armstrong. Call It Courage   97
    Stone, Nancy. Dune Shadow   131
    Taylor, Theodore. Cay, The   131
    Townsend, John Rowe. Dan Alone   131
    Truss, Jan. Jasmin   146

WARS
  --Civil War
    Hunt, Irene. Across Five Aprils   155
    Hurmence, Belinda. Tancy   155
    Keith, Harold. Rifles for Watie   156
    Lunn, Janet. Root Cellar, The   158
    Steele, William O. Perilous Road, The   130
  --French and Indian
    Edmonds, Walter. Matchlock Gun, The   71
  --Revolutionary
    Brady, Esther Wood. Toliver's Secret   69
    Collier, James Lincoln and Christopher. My Brother Sam Is
       Dead   150; War Comes to Willy Freeman   150
    Forbes, Esther. Johnny Tremain   152
  --Shays' Rebellion
    Collier, James Lincoln and Christopher. Winter Hero, The
       150
  --War of 1812
    Brady, Esther Wood. Toad on Capitol Hill, The   82
  --World War I
    Mukerji, Dhan Gopal. Gay-Neck; The Story of a Pigeon
       159
  --World War II
    Anderson, Margaret J. Searching for Shona   81
    Bawden, Nina. Carrie's War   116
    Cooper, Susan. Dawn of Fear   138